As L'Amour stood there, he himself looked like a character out of some of his own novels. Over six feet tall, weighing over 200 pounds, barrel-chested and with a square, weathered face, his eyes were deep set and hazel, his curly hair dark. As he gestured, one could not help but notice that his hands were massive and strong, like those of a cattleman or a miner. L'Amour had been both. In his gait he was big, expansive, and lumbering. He punched the air for emphasis.

It was clear he identified with his fictional heroes, who were also big.

L'Amour remained confident that when future historians and critics look back on what elements made the West, his books will be considered seminal sources. "I hope that someday people will look at me and realize what an amazing thing I did." Modesty was not always his forte. "I don't know if any writer has ever taken on the scope I've taken on. I am trying to bring the West's history out of the myths from the very beginning."

BOOKS BY ROBERT PHILLIPS

Biography/Criticism
LOUIS L'AMOUR: HIS LIFE AND TRAILS
WILLIAM GOYEN
DENTON WELCH
THE CONFESSIONAL POETS

Poetry
INNER WEATHER
THE PREGNANT MAN
RUNNING ON EMPTY
PERSONAL ACCOUNTS
THE WOUNDED ANGEL

Fiction
THE LAND OF LOST CONTENT

Anthologies/Editions
ASPECTS OF ALICE
THE STORIES OF DENTON WELCH
THE COLLECTED STORIES OF
  NOEL COWARD
LETTERS OF DELMORE SCHWARTZ
LAST & LOST POEMS OF DELMORE
  SCHWARTZ
THE EGO IS ALWAYS AT THE WHEEL:
  Bagatelles by Delmore Schwartz
MOONSTRUCK: An Anthology of Lunar
  Poetry

LOUIS L'AMOUR: HIS LIFE AND TRAILS

ROBERT PHILLIPS

KNIGHTSBRIDGE PUBLISHING COMPANY

NEW YORK

DEDICATED TO ELINOR S. ELLIS—
WHO PUSHED ME TO NEW FRONTIERS.

This paperback edition of *Louis L'Amour: His Life and Trails* first published in 1990 by Knightsbridge Publishing Company

Originally published by Paperjacks Ltd. in 1989

Published in the United States by
Knightsbridge Publishing Company
255 East 49th Street
New York, New York 10017

ISBN: 1-877961-12-4

10 9 8 7 6 5 4 3 2 1

FIRST EDITION

TABLE OF CONTENTS

FOREWORD 1

PROLOGUE 7

CHAPTER ONE
   Childhood 13

CHAPTER TWO
   Youth 43

CHAPTER THREE
   Fame........................ 77

CHAPTER FOUR
   Family 101

CHAPTER FIVE
   Old Age..................... 171

EPILOGUE 193

BIBLIOGRAPHY, CHECKLISTS 213

To dream is in the mind,
the realization in the hands.

—Louis L'Amour,
To the Far Blue Mountains (1976)

FOREWORD

The life of Louis L'Amour neatly breaks into two halves. The first half could come directly out of some of his own books of high adventure—*Killoe* or *Kilrone*—rough years when L'Amour was often hungry, out of work, and facing the situations he has written about. These were his "yondering" years, to use a verb he himself coined, years in which he wandered yonder. Completely unknown during these decades, the events in his life are fairly well documented through L'Amour's autobiographical notes, interviews, encyclopedic references, family records, and publicity blurbs.

The second half of his life, after L'Amour became famous, or at least very wealthy and known to a huge cult, is totally different. He chose what he has called "the almost monastic life": daily writing in the morning, exercising in the afternoon, and reading in the evening. He had to live that simply to fulfill his ambitions and his contractual obligations. He agreed to a publishing schedule of three books a year for many years. Fortunately, he was not a social gadfly. L'Amour generally avoided the social scene, only emerging now and then to travel to promote a new book. So, paradoxically, there is at present much less available material on L'Amour's years of fame—roughly, from the publication of *Hondo* in 1953 on—than there is on his years of obscurity.

This book, then, is an effort to begin to document the life of that man obsessed with pioneers. There are no claims to it being the definitive biography. Others will and should follow, as one hopes L'Amour's own autobiography will follow, as promised. In a letter to an academic, dated January 18, 1984, he stated that he was in the midst of writing a two-volume autobiography. However, in an interview just a year earlier, the author stated his reluctance to write one. "I'm not sure I could recapture the way I was or the way I thought ... It's hard to get those feelings back again, because I don't feel that way anymore." One obituary stated that he had finished reading proofs of his autobiography in his last hours. In all probability, he did tackle the book in some form; he once said he had ideas going for 45 books simultaneously!

In either event, this book is a beginning at documenting the life that produced over 190 million books in print around the world, the man whom the *Washington Post* called "the General Motors of Westerns," and others called "the Laureate of the Lariat." According to Bantam Books publicity releases, if all the L'Amour books in print were stacked flat on top of one another, the stack would reach more than 1,100 miles into outer space. That is a statistic that would have greatly pleased Louis L'Amour, who strongly believed that nature had no use for non-producers. "I love to tell stories and I have a lot more to tell. I can't imagine not working," he said.

For genealogical and biographical facts, I am grateful to many sources listed in the back matter of this book. But I wish to pay special thanks to Robert L. Gale for his book, *Louis L'Amour* (Twayne Publishers, Boston, 1985). While his is ostensibly the first book of literary criticism to be written about L'Amour, his chapters and notes are full of LaMoore and L'Amour family information, which he gleaned from family members, correspondence and scrapbooks, as well as his own footwork in and around Jamestown, North Dakota.

I would also like to thank Fredda Feldman and John Wyatt for aiding me in researching this book during one of the hottest summers in recorded history.

R.P.

PROLOGUE

It was, for some, a strange scene. The date was September 24, 1983. The place was outside the White House in Washington, D.C. The President of the United States was personally presiding over the ceremony. The honored were the Professional Rodeo Cowboys Association, members of which stood by with hands clasped behind their backs. They wore ten-gallon hats, and pointed cowboy boots. They wore string neckties and turquoise belt buckles. Members of the Association had performed for the President before the ceremony, and afterward, there would be a barbecue on the South Lawn.

But the guest of honor was another cowboy, Louis L'Amour. He was to be presented the Congressional Gold Medal, which up to that time had been awarded to only 70 individuals. The first recipient was George Washington. L'Amour was also the first American novelist to receive the medal—not Mark Twain, Herman Melville, Nathaniel Hawthorne, Henry James, William Faulkner, Ernest Hemingway or Saul Bellow. The only other literary figure to receive it was the poet Robert Frost. And Robert Frost was one of the most political men who ever lived.

L'Amour was standing in the audience, looking like all the other participants with his braided-leather bolo tie and his Western belt buckle. When the time in the program came for him to receive his medal, President Ronald Reagan requested that he come forward. In anticipation, the President turned left. But the seventy-one-year-old L'Amour made his way forward from behind the President, looking for all the world like a paunchy, over-the-hill cowboy. The President turned and started. Then he blurted out, "Well . . . there you are. You sneaked up on me, like, like—you know—Bowdrie."

How L'Amour could be voted this high honor, and how the President of the United States could cite the name of L'Amour's Texas Ranger character ad lib, is what this book is all about. At the time, he received the award, L'Amour had written 87 books—all but one a Western. His sales had totalled 190 million. That not only made him the best-selling Western writer ever, but that he outsold the next ten or fifteen contenders combined!

CHAPTER ONE

CHILDHOOD

Louis L'Amour. The name itself sounds highly improbable for the author of Western and adventure novels. As one of his early editors said, L'Amour on a paperback sounded like "a Western written in lipstick." It even sounds made-up, contrived, like the name of a 1930s motion picture matinee idol.

Yet the name is, in fact, a variant spelling of his real given name, LaMoore. In a 1982 interview in *American West*, L'Amour claimed his family name had always been L'Amour; his father had changed it to LaMoore because people were always spelling it wrong. When Louis became a published author, he went back to the original L'Amour.

But like many of the "facts" in his interviews, this claim is difficult to support. A born romantic, the man probably just liked the looks and connotations of "L'Amour". Its French roots complemented the name Louis, not to mention its meaning related to *love*. As a television character recently said, "I'm a sucker for music, romance, and indirect lighting." Perhaps L'Amour was, too.

For whatever reason, like the novelists Nathaniel Hawthorne, Herman Melville, and William Faulkner, L'Amour chose to change the spelling of his last name. Then for a time afterward, he was reluctant to use it in print, saying, "No editor believed the name 'L'Amour' could ever appear on a Western story." This accounts for his early pennames "Tex Burns" and "Jim Mayo". All his life, he was name-conscious: in *Mojave Crossing* (1964), he writes, "It sounds like a made-up name, but I'd known folks with real names that sounded made-up." Like L'Amour.

Louis Dearborn L'Amour was a 10th-generation American. His father was Louis Charles LaMoore (1868-1952); his mother was Emily Louis Dearborn LaMoore (1870-1954). The family was of French-Irish stock, and L'Amour carefully traced his American ancestry as far back as the 1630s. He was greatly interested in genealogy, and in later life L'Amour would be the recipient of the National Genealogical Society Award. He also managed to trace his wife's English and Scottish roots, and relished the fact that both sets of ancestors had lived at one time in the same small village with a population of less than three thousand people. "They couldn't have missed knowing each other—I was fascinated at the thought that a lot of Americans are married or are good friends whose ancestors might have known each other under dramatic circumstances. Perhaps they suffered together through that terrible winter at Valley Forge," he mused in a piece in *Reader's Digest*, "or traveled on the same wagon-train trek."

In all probability, the fact that his and his wife's families' lives intertwined accounts for the sagas of his fictional Sacketts, Talons and Chantrys, whose generations brush elbows with one another and intermarry over a period of forty years. They, too, came separately to this country from the British Isles and northwestern France.

Louis L'Amour's forebears were pioneering types on both sides of the family. He listed sodbusters, trappers, cavalrymen, cowboys—and possibly an Indian or two—as ancestors. On his father's side his grandfather, Rober L'Moore, was born in Ontario. His ancestors were French Huguenot refugees from Ireland who emigrated to Canada. Their name at that time may have been Larmour. Robert L'Moore married Angelina LaDoux, a French-Canadian from Montreal. L'Moore changed his name to Moore when he came to the States. He saw action in the Civil War and later settled in Michigan.

Robert L'Moore and his wife had twin sons, one of whom was named Louis Charles, who became the novelist's father. The twins were born on February 29, 1868, a Leap Year. An infant sister died—as did their mother—when the twins were quite young. Louis L'Amour's father, consequently, was reared in Ontario by paternal grandparents. Upon leaving secondary school, he began studies for a career in veterinary medicine in Guelph, Ontario and completed later in South Dakota. He had a great love and compassion for animals which he would pass on to his son.

On his mother's side, L'Amour is descended from Ambrose ("Ambros", in one printed account) Truman Freeman, his great-grandfather, who was an anti-slavery Virginian, later transplanted to Illinois. During the Civil War, Freeman joined the Union Army and then went to Minneapolis. Later, he fought against the Indians with the Sibley Expedition far out in the Dakota plains. Freeman was killed and scalped by a Sioux war party. There are several published accounts of this killing, the best by George F. Brackett, who was with Freeman at the time, but managed to escape with his life. The event occurred on July 24, 1863, near what is known today as Pettibone, North Dakota.

Louis L'Amour, as a teenager and young man, loved to tell and tell again the tale of his murdered Indian-fighter, Great-Grand-father Freeman, as well as the skirmishes in which his Grandfather L'Moore partici-pated. The scalping is retold in many of his interviews. L'Amour dedicated *Kiowa Trail* to the memory of Ambrose Freeman, and this great-grandfather plays an offstage role in *Taggart*. Clearly the man was an exemplar, a true original.

Also on L'Amour's maternal side was an American Revolutionary War army sur-geon named Levi Dearborn. He hailed from New Hampshire and was educated at Har-vard. He had a great love of books.

Dr. Dearborn had a brother, General Henry Dearborn, who served as Secretary of State under Thomas Jefferson. So Louis L'Amour was not the first of his family to be entertained in the White House. General Henry Dearborn was a great keeper of diaries, the subjects of which included the battle of Bunker Hill, Valley Forge, the second battle of Saratoga, Cornwallis' sur-render, and Arnold's march to Quebec. General Henry Dearborn had a son who wrote a dozen books, including a biography of Admiral Bainbridge and a naval history of the Black Sea. The biography of Admiral

Bainbridge, who commanded the *Constitution*, was not published until the 1930s, when it was brought out by Princeton University Press.

Dr. Dearborn's son, Levi Dearborn, Jr., also a gentleman and a reader, moved to Pennsylvania in his adult years. And his son, Abraham Dearborn, pioneered all the way out to Minnesota and later saw combat with the Union Army during the Civil War. He served with the Third Minnesota Division, and fought valiantly until his regiment surrendered at Murfreesboro, Tennessee.

Abraham Dearborn and Ambrose Freeman both had been skirmishing with the Sioux Indians. They were fated to meet on the Dakota-Minnesota border, and eventually, the two men became good friends. When Freeman took the bachelor Dearborn home to St. Cloud, Minnesota, to meet his pretty daughter, Elizabeth (Betty) Freeman, the two fell in love. Perhaps Freeman knew the two young people would hit it off. Abraham and Elizabeth were married in Illinois in July, 1864.

This marriage produced three daughters, the third of which, Emily Lavisa Dearborn, was born in 1870, six years after the marriage. She would become the mother of Louis L'Amour. Her father, Abraham, would come to live with the couple and be a great storytelling influence on the future novelist.

Emily's mother, Betty Freeman, from all accounts—and there are many—was a pretty and loyal pioneer woman, a true gentlewoman. She has even been the subject of a couple of books, most notably, *Yet She Follows: The Story of Betty Freeman*, written by Edna LaMoore Waldo (Capital Publishing Company, Bismarck, N.D., 1931).

After their marriage, Abraham and Elizabeth LaMoore moved to Jamestown, North Dakota in 1884. It was in Jamestown where Emily first met Louis Charles LaMoore. LaMoore had come to the town North Dakota town of Ellendale. Emily and Louis were married in 1892. The marriage produced seven children, two of whom were twins and died as infants. Another child died as a teenage victim of the flu epidemic. The LaMoore children were Edna May LaMoore Waldo, author of the book on Betty Freeman as well as other volumes (born in 1893); Charles Parker LaMoore (1897-1954); Yale Freeman ("Bill") LaMoore

(1899-1954); Emmy Louis LaMoore (1901-1919); and Clara and Clarice LaMoore (1903-1904).

Louis Dearborn L'Amour, destined to become the Dean of Western Writers, was born on March 22, 1908. Gale's book is the only source where the exact day of L'Amour's birth is given. All other reference books list only the year, even those references to which L'Amour himself contributed. Perhaps this is one of L'Amour's quirks. Certainly, he had one about revealing his age. He became very secretive about the subject of his age sometime about the period when he reached his late sixties or early seventies. L'Amour once wrote a friend that the reason he concealed his age was in order to be able to appeal to younger readers; if they thought he was a fossil, they wouldn't listen to his voice. Gale suggested that he wanted people to think he began his writing career earlier than he, in fact, did. L'Amour was forty-two years old when his first novel appeared—an age when many people have already achieved their life goals.

Another theory is that he concealed his age because he married so late in life—at the age of forty-six—and was approaching middle age when his two children were born when he was in his fifties. Toward the end of his life, L'Amour would allow only to being "slightly younger" than President Reagan. This evasiveness about age was most likely a matter of vanity or egocentricity. He loved to dress in cowboy garb to be photographed. He loved to relive the adventures of his youth, and he identified with his own characters, who were physically tough. Reporters and interviewers frequently wrote admiringly of his six-foot-two-inch height, his still dark brown-grey hair, his good looks, and his good physical condition for an older man.

L'Amour told one interviewer, "I spent my first years making people think I was older than I really was; now I'm working just as hard at keeping people from guessing my age."

As early as 1956, when he was forty-eight years old, he told another interviewer, "I never mention my age to anybody at all. I don't think anybody ever should, no matter who they are. I stopped telling my age as a philosophical thing as well as a kind of protest."

The article goes on to explain that when L'Amour was eighteen, he worked on construction jobs, lumber camps, and mining camps—work that necessitated physical strength. In Oregon, he worked beside two men, one a millwright (a super carpenter) and the other a carpenter. One man was thirty years old, the other man, forty-two. L'Amour admired them both for their skill and efficiency. He recognized that the two men were better workers than he could ever be.

"We went to apply for a job at an oil company, and guess who got the job?" L'Amour said with indignation, raising his peaked eyebrows. "They turned these two men down because they said they were too old. I was going to be a writer. I knew it even then. Yet this was their livelihood. They weren't going to do anything else for the rest of their lives. When they turned away from that counter, their faces were grey with shock. I stood there, thinking how terribly, terribly unjust it was that they were turned down just because of an idea about age."

L'Amour went on here—and elsewhere—to say that age has no bearing on anything. He pointed out that William Pitt was England's Chancellor of the Exchequer when he was twenty-three. Conversely, if Winston

Churchill had died when he was sixty-five, he would never have gone down in history as amounting to much. "So there's no telling, you see," L'Amour concluded. "Some men mature late and come into themselves late; others arrive very early. Age has nothing to do with it." It was a very sore point.

In addition to sisters Edna and Emmy and brothers Charles and Yale ("Bill"), young Louis was joined by another sibling—an orphaned New York City boy named John Otto. John was sent west with a trainload of orphans and other unwanted children. The LaMoores took pity on him, and John supplanted Louis as the youngest child in the family. He was reported to be an unattractive boy, largely due to having crossed eyes. But the LaMoores loved him as their very own, and eventually had an operation performed on John's eyes to correct this problem.

The LaMoore house was situated in the valley where the Pipestem River and the James River meet. It was a small frame house located in the middle of town. Known locally as Doc LaMoore, Louis' father was a practicing veterinarian for the state as well as keeping up his private practice. In his spare time, he also sold and repaired farm machinery, mostly steam threshers and tractors. A Methodist, he taught Sunday School every week for years. He was also very active in civic affairs, and served as city councilman, local juvenile commissioner, town alderman, and both county and state delegate for the Republican party. Doc LaMoore was also an unsuccessful candidate in his bid for mayor.

As if all this were not enough, he held the office of local park planner, and was a deputy sheriff. In the latter capacity, he got into several fist fights, and became a kind of hero around town. This notoriety gave Louis a very special status with the other boys. He took pride that his father actually fought with his fists. L'Amour once said, "Whenever there was a crime, my father just put out the word that the wrongdoers had better ride in and give themselves up and they usually did. Dad could be pretty tough if he had to go out after a man."[1]

1. *Writer's Digest*, Dec. 1960

Doc LaMoore was both strong and athletic, and perhaps Louis inherited his energy and ability to compartmentalize his time from his father. One thing he definitely passed along to Louis was his love of boxing. He taught all three sons how to box, a skill Louis later would develop to a high degree. His father also loved animals—a natural affinity for a veterinarian—and the LaMoore home had both horses and dogs on the premises. Louis learned how to ride at an early age.

His mother, Emily, had gone to normal school, a teacher's college, in St. Cloud, Minnesota, in preparation for a career as an educator. But once she met Doc LaMoore, those ambitions were put behind her. She never relinquished her fondness of books and writing, however. She read widely, was said to be a good storyteller, and wrote poetry. Perhaps she influenced the creation of Louis' first published book, which was not a novel at all, but rather a collection of poems—and rather a bad one at that. Mrs. LaMoore's other interest was gardening, in which she is reported to have engaged "with a passion". As Gale observed, "L'Amour obviously inherited a combination of physical strength and intelligent sensitivity from his parents."

Jamestown, the place where young Louis grew up, is in the southeast quarter of North Dakota. It is the county seat of Stutsman County. In those days, it was still rugged country, and Doc LaMoore had dealings with many of the Indians in the area. Jamestown was settled in 1872 by the construction crews of the Northern Pacific Railway. These crews were protected from hostile Indians by soldiers from Ft. Seward between 1872, until the fort was abandoned, and 1877. Because of its river location, Jamestown became a transportation and trade center for that part of the state. Livestock and wheat were produced in abundance on the farms of North Dakota.

At the time of Louis' birth, the town population was around 7,000. In those days Jamestown boasted of flour mills—four in number—grain elevators, and stockyards. North of town is the Jamestown Dam, on the James River, which provides water for irrigation, flood protection, and a place for recreation. Louis and his brothers used to swim in the James River. Jamestown is a town one can imagine populated by plain-speaking, straight-shooting heroes, like the ones who populate L'Amour's stories—a town visited by itinerant preachers, miners, gunslingers, cattle barons, and mountain men.

Also located in the town is Jamestown College, which was established in 1886. Eighty-six years later, in 1972, the college awarded Jamestown's favorite son an Honorary LL.D. By then, Louis L'Amour had become known as "The Dean of Western Writers," and it was only appropriate for a Dean to have a Doctorate degree. The "Dean" designation, however, was one he did not think much of. As he told a staff reporter of the *Wall Street Journal*, "If you write a book set in the past about something that happened east of the Mississippi, it's a historical novel. If you write about something that took place west of the Mississippi, it's a Western, and somehow regarded as a lesser work. I write historical novels about the frontier."

L'Amour's later paperbacks carried such subtitles as, "Stories by the World's Best-selling Frontier Author," and "Frontier Stories Personally Selected and Introduced by the Author." He was, by choice, a "frontier author", not a "Western author". Some books overrode the issue entirely by proclaiming, "Tales by America's Favorite Storyteller."

In the electronic age of television, it is difficult today to realize just how important story-telling was in the home, in those days. As an adult, L'Amour had fond recollections of visitors to his childhood home, the family and visitors all sitting around the kitchen table while he listened, enraptured. No doubt, this is the intimate feeling he attempted to recapture when, decades later, he would read to his own children at the breakfast table.

In *American West* he recollected, "I had an uncle by marriage. He married my mother's oldest sister. He was an interesting man. I only remember him as a fella who visited us occasionally when I was a small boy. He had managed a ranch right outside The Hole in the Wall. And Butch Cassidy and the Sundance Kid used to ride across his pasture going to The Hole in the Wall. Sometimes they'd be in a hurry and stop at his corral. They'd leave their horses and take his. He never minded because the horses they left were usually better than his . . ."

This uncle and L'Amour's aunt wandered all the way from British Columbia to Sonora, Mexico. They managed a sizeable cattle ranch in the Star Valley of Wyoming, and drove a RFD mail route.

Such tales fueled the young boy's imagination. Besides his maternal uncle, his grandfather Lt. Abraham Dearborn was also a mentor and great storyteller. Louis' sister, Edna, found the grandfather to be too reserved, too cold. But he seemed quite different around Louis, perhaps because Louis was a boy. He let the old man regale him with stories of Indian fighting and the battles of the Civil War he fought with the Third Minnesota Division. The grandfather would diagram military tactics and strategies on a blackboard for the boy, describing how all the great battles of history had been won or lost—talk that was infinitely boring to Edna but wildly exciting to Louis. Every Memorial Day, the grandfather would dress in his old blue army uniform, complete with sashes, and participate in the parade festivities. The boy was greatly impressed.

Louis was also all ears when some of his grandfather's Indian acquaintances, with whom he had fought out West, would drop by the house when passing through Jamestown. They would sip coffee together in the kitchen and discuss battle tactics and argue about why the winners had won and the losers had lost in each particular battle. This was some of the boy's first contact with Indians, and he could see they were not exotic "others," but scrappers like his own grandfather. The stories he heard in his home became a part of him. By the age of twelve, he said, he knew that writing was something he wanted to do.

When his sister Emmy Louis died— L'Amour said she was only seventeen, others say she was nineteen—she had written a lot of poetry. "I think in my own heart she would have been another Edna St. Vincent Millay. She was that good," Louis wrote years later. So, in addition to his mother, his sister was an influence toward L'Amour's penchant for poetic prose. His sentences contain many similes and a good amount of metaphors. His prose is also known to adopt a rhythmic stance. His images, unfortunately, are rarely original. Many come from games of cards. Gale catalogued the four most recurring images in his prose as a.) describing rain like a mesh of metal, b.) creek water as chuckling, c.) stars as lamps, and d.) stealthy movements as ghostlike. L'Amour was also given to poetic inversions in his prose, in such sentences as, "Green lay the coast and gray the sea."

But there was an undeniable literary affinity in his family. His brother Parker LaMoore wrote one book, and was a newspaperman all his life. As chief editorial writer for Scripps-Howard, he is reported to have covered all the Big Four Conferences during World War II. There were not only books all around the LaMoore house; the children also grew up wanting to write books. L'Amour later claimed that since 1816, thirty-three members of his family had been writers!

In *The Lonesome Gods* L'Amour wrote, "How young is too young to begin to discover the power and the beauty of words? Perhaps he will not understand, but there is a clash and a call of trumpets in these lines. One cannot begin too young nor linger too long with learning." In another interview, he claimed he had "wanted to write almost from the time he would walk."

In the first grade, a teacher asked Louis what he wanted to be when he grew up. He answered, "A scientist"—but that wasn't what he was thinking about. Had he known the name, he might have replied, "A philosopher," for that was closer to the things he wanted to write about. He told Michael T. Marsden that what he really wanted to do was to write about people.

Everybody in the LaMoore family did a great deal of reading. The LaMoore family library numbered 300 volumes—a rarity in those days. In addition, there was a good public library in Jamestown, the Alfred Dickey Library, to which every member of the family had a card. They would return home weekly with arms full of books. Louis recalled devouring the library shelves as if they held food and he was starving.

One of Louis' particular favorites as a child was Robert Louis Stevenson's *Treasure Island*. He also read several of Sir Walter Scott's books, including *Ivanhoe*. He once said that Scott had the most profound influence upon the West of any writer that had ever lived. Scott's ideas of chivalry, he thought, influenced the behavior of cowboys, most of whom had read him. Cowboys, for instance, would never harm a woman travelling alone. "It's hard to believe that a decent woman could ride anywhere in the West entirely alone and be unmolested and safe. Rape was almost unknown," L'Amour mused in *American West*.

Gale compiled a partial list of L'Amour's favorite reading, which was gleaned from many sources. That list includes Balzac, Bulwer-Lytton, Chaqucer, Dickens, Dostoevsky, Zane Grey, O. Henry, Jack London, Marx, Maupassant, Mill, Poe, Shakespeare, Tolstoy, and Trollope. He also read Washington Irving and the poets Robinson Jeffers and Longfellow. Before he was twelve, he had read forty Dumas novels, several by Hugo, *Scotish Chiefs* by Porter, *Westward Ho* by Kingsley, and much of Stevenson and DeFoe. Much of what he read, he retained.

At an early age he drew pictures of cowboys and Indians, cut them out, and used them as characters in little dramas in which he participated. L'Amour seems to have been born with wanderlust. He would trace out routes on the maps of his geography books, routes for future travels he intended to make. As an adolescent, he began to hang around bookstores, wherever he could find them.

L'Amour's respect for the Indians went beyond his encounters with his grandfather's redskin acquaintances around the kitchen table. As a boy of four or five, he accompanied his father to an Indian camp. The most marvelous sound he'd heard, he thought at that time, was the laughter of the old squaws, sitting around a campfire, chuckling in rich, deep tones. He thought that the Indians were very vibrant and alive. L'Amour stated that the only reason they got a reputation for being stoical "was that some white man came along and asked them some stupid question".[2]

At the age of twelve, he visited an uncle in Minnesota, and experienced one of his first scares in the great outdoors he grew to love and respect. Back home in the prairie state

2. Marsden, "A Conversation with Louis L'Amour"

of North Dakota, trees were found only along the rivers or in tree claims. Here in the dense Minnesota forests, he attempted a three-mile walk alone and got lost. At any moment, he expected to encounter a bear. It was in this apprehensive state of mind that he surprised a cluster of resting partridges. The birds took off in a loud flurry, frightening the boy. Louis was greatly relieved when he found his way back to his uncle's house.

That same year, Louis visited his brother, Parker, in Oklahoma City, while his parents remained in North Dakota. On the trip he read a penny dreadful Western, *The Passing of the Oklahoma Outlaw*, written by a famous marshall, Bill Tilghman. Two days after the boy's arrival in Oklahoma City, Bill Tilghman, himself, came to call on Louis' brother. "It was every kid's dream, talking to an ex-marshall of Dodge City who had ridden against the Dalton gang." Tilghman was retired as a frontier marshall, but still worked as an Oklahoma state police officer. It was his job to transport prisoners from jail to the penitentiary. He was still an expert marksman, despite his advancing years. The boys begged Tilghman to teach them how to shoot.

Tilghman took the two brothers out to the canyon where the North Canadian River runs through Oklahoma City. For this demonstration, he'd brought along a single-action Colt Peacemaker .45. From thirty paces, he shot the pips off a deck of cards. "Then, as if to show us what real shooting was, he split a card edgewise with a bullet," L'Amour wrote in *Gun World*. On his "60 Minutes" TV appearance on CBS in 1976, he repeated the advice Tilghman had given him that day: "Make the first shot count—you may never get another one!"

Bill Tilghman was gunned down about a year after that afternoon. He had been investigating a dope ring in the Oklahoma oil fields. Wiley Lynn, a paid gunman for the dope ring, pretended to be a playful drunk in a dancehall Tilghman frequented. Lynn—a non-drinker—had the odor of alcohol on his shirt and waved around a flashy pistol. Tilghman took the gun away from him and escorted him outside the hall. It never occurred to him to search the man. Once outside, Lynn produced a second gun and shot Tilghman dead. After a trial, Lynn was somehow acquitted. L'Amour wrote that he thought a lot of money was behind the defence.

During his twelfth year, Louis read his first book of non-fiction, *The Genius of Solitude* —solitude was to play an important role in his life, ever after. Between the years of twelve and fifteen, Louis read many non-fiction books, particularly those on topics such as botany, natural history, geology, mineralogy, history and military science. He read Edward Gibbon's *History of the Decline and Fall of the Roman Empire*, as well as treatises on aircraft and submarines. He studied kites and hot air balloons. "I often fell asleep reading," he recollected in *The Roundup* magazine. "My mother would take the book from my hands and put it on the table." This is a tender tableau, and one completely at odds with the rough-and-tumble life he was to begin within the year.

Louis held a variety of part-time jobs as a boy. At the age of twelve, he was a Western Union messenger. When he was fourteen years old, he began to box, sparring with professionals. This was an activity he would return to at various times in his life.

Despite his love of books, he wasn't much for compartmentalized schooling. At the age of fifteen, he dropped out and never attended school beyond the tenth grade. How much of this was due to economic pressure, would be difficult to assume.

The Midwest was experiencing economic hardship during 1923. There was more competition for sales of farm machinery, but few buyers. Doc LaMoore's customers were farmers who had gone broke and couldn't manage to pay their bills. The elder LaMoore was in financial trouble. He sold the home in North Dakota and moved his family to the Southwest, looking for a better life. According to Gale, "Young Louis soon decided not to be a burden on the family and struck out, irregularly at first, on his own, returned to his parents again, and left again, soon beginning to hold an incredible sequence of educative jobs." One biographical article has him packing just one change of clothes and a dozen books to take with him on the road.

But there are other versions. In one of the most dramatic of these stories, Louis went to visit the older brother, Parker LaMoore, in Oklahoma the summer he was fifteen. Parker was private secretary to Oklahoma Governor, M.E. Tripp. The plan was for Louis to join his parents in New Mexico after seeing his brother. But when the boy arrived in New Mexico, they already had moved on. According to one interview, Louis took this as a signal to strike out on his own. Which he did. He didn't attempt to catch up with his parents, and did not see them for a long time. They were, however, reunited in the late 1930s in Oklahoma City. And when he began to write fiction, many of his heroes would be rawboned kids who are, literally, teenage orphans. Which must have been how he felt at the time.

It is probable that the discovery that his family was suddenly poverty-stricken, traumatized the boy. Certainly, it may go a long way toward explaining why, decades later, with millions in the bank, he would continue to grind out a total of three books a year, 101 in all. He may have been overcompensating for the impoverished boy and the financially embarrassed father.

CHAPTER TWO

YOUTH

Louis L'Amour did what most every young boy dreams of and would like to do—he actually ran away from home and joined the circus. His job was to handle the elephants. For this he was paid breakfast money. The circus took him throughout Arizona and Texas. (In later accounts, L'Amour claimed the circus toured Siam!) But after only a few weeks he quit the circus, hopped freight trains, and hired out as a ranch hand in West Texas.

One early job he took was skinning dead cattle. "The cattle," L'Amour said, "had a smell to high heaven. Many of them had been dead for weeks, you know. It was the only job available, though, and I was lucky to get anything—I was down to my last bit of eating money."

The best part of that job, L'Amour told *American Way* magazine, was the old man who had hired him. He was seventy-odd years old and strong. He had been captured by the Apaches when he was seven, and was brought up as one of them. When he reached nineteen years of age, he left to punch cows in Texas, but returned and lived among the Apaches for ten more years, both in Mexico and in the mountains of Sierre Madre.

"I . . . I had a real prize in the old man. Today I'd know many more questions to ask him. Then, I didn't know the questions. Mostly I listened . . . There was nobody to interrupt us . . . Once in a while, some cowboy would stop off to the windward of us, you know, and talk a little bit. The smell was pretty bad; it was weeks before I got it out of my nostrils, after I left the job . . . Every evening and every morning,

every lunchtime—whenever we'd stop—
we'd talk, and much of it was about the
country and the Indians. So I had a chance
to learn a lot."

L'Amour was paid three dollars a day to
skin all the dead cattle on that rancher's
spread. There were, by his account, 925 car-
casses in all. Despite the sickening stench,
he stayed until the last one was skinned,
listening avidly to the old man. The codger
spun tales about riding with the great war
chiefs and fighting the white man. Louis
received valuable first-hand material which
he would utilize later in *Hondo*, *Shalako*,
and *Sky-Liners*. It was a rare opportunity to
hear about the Indians from an insider's
point-of-view.

When he was eighteen, he found himself
dealing with dead bodies of another sort—
the human variety. He worked part-time for
an undertaker. It was his job to clean up the
bodies of those who were victims of fights
the night before.

Other odd jobs followed. He became a
hay cutter and baler in New Mexico, working in the Pecos Valley. Later, he was a
flume builder and a fruit picker. He worked
around Ft. Sumner, Ruidoso, Socorro, Las

Vegas, Santa Rosa, and Las Cruces. "I never punched cows, but a lot of my friends did," he told Harold Keith. "When I was around Kingman, Arizona, several of my friends were cowpunchers from the Big Sandy. I went to dances with them, less for the dancing than the fighting." He appeared to enjoy a good row.

The years between the ages of fifteen and eighteen were not easy ones for L'Amour. He often went hungry and even spent some nights in jail as a result of his fighting. Other nights, he slept in lumber piles with newspapers wrapped under his coat to keep warm. Still other nights found him sleeping in empty box cars—if he was lucky enough to find one—or inside abandoned buildings. He could never be certain if his companion across the darkened room was a cat or a rat.

One time L'Amour found himself in a pirogue (a dugout canoe), being taken through the bayous of southern Louisiana by a Cajun guide. He noticed the waters were populated by cottonmouth water moccasins which are very poisonous snakes. Once he got lost in the Mohave Desert and despaired of ever getting out. Working in the lumberyards of the Northwest, he did some felling of trees and topping trees, as well. Some were giant chesnuts and tulip trees a dozen feet in girth. He quit the job because he no longer wanted to participate in the logging of trees that it had taken nature hundreds of years to grow. This reveals the young man's sensitivity and ecological awareness—an awareness he would retain all his life. He always built his camp fires where someone else had built one, to trespass on nature less. He never would kill a grizzly bear, he said, because there are too few of them left.

This concern for ecology is reflected in the books he was to write. In *Jubal Sackett*, for example, a son recalls his father: "There was never a place he walked that was not the better for his having passed. For every tree he cut down, he planted two." Throughout L'Amour's books one finds the notion that we humans only hold the land in trust for the generations ahead, our sons and their sons.

As a drifter, L'Amour was lucky to take mining work when it was available. What he liked doing most was assessment work on mining claims, even though, it meant being alone much of the time. Working in the Monte Cristo Mountains of Nevada, he shoveled or trammed—pushing an ore cart that held up to a ton of ore. Assessment work was hard physical work, which was needed to develop a mining property and bring it closer to production. When assessing, L'Amour had to drill, blast, and muck out ore—tough work, indeed.

After work hours, he liked to hike along the mountains and take in the scenery which included views of the Big Smokey Valley. Usually he took his time, not hurrying anywhere. He would rather know a small area very well than try to cover larger areas superficially. He had found the way to see the local animal life was by remaining quiet in one place, for a long time. Once, he came face to face with a huge bighorn ram. Another time, retracking his steps back to the mine, he realized he had been followed by a mountain lion.

L'Amour claimed never to be much of a cook. Most of the time, he ate from a can and boiled coffee cowboy-style, in a small tin pot that made only two cups. Once he joked about frontier coffee in his book *Conagher*, writing, "They like it strong out here. They say if you can't float a horseshoe on it the coffee is too weak." Sometimes he travelled light and didn't carry canned food at all. Then he ate nuts, dried fruit, or hard candy. The candy, he thought, quenched his thirst and was a good source of energy. When hiking alone, he sometimes would go an entire day without eating. He didn't like to cook, really, and welcomed a partner to do it for him. But that had its disadvantages; a partner would probably want to talk which would break the young man's solitude and communion with nature.

Like many of his novels' protagonists, L'Amour would read by campfire after his simple meal was eaten. He learned the wisdom of shaking out his boots in the morning before putting them on. This was a landscape of rattlesnakes and tarantulas, and either could be lying in wait. When one mine owner asked him how he could stand to be alone so much of the time, L'Amour replied, "I wasn't alone. I had a mountain with me."

He was nineteen years old when he and a friend came to the San Juan Mountains of

Colorado. They had ridden the train from Durango to Silverton and their object was to get another job in the mines, but they had no such luck. Taking the train back, they got off at Needleton where his friend had a mining claim above Johnson Creek, in Vallecito Canyon. L'Amour wanted to catch up on his assessment work so the two young men hiked into the Chicago Basin and camped out. Others were in the same area, some prospecting for gold, others working claims. L'Amour helped his friend with the necessary assessment work, but spent most of these days sightseeing. He had saved some money and felt as if he could take some time off to enjoy the high mountain country—which he liked the best, of all the places he had ever seen. L'Amour climbed to Hidden Lake and hiked around Irving Peak. He saw Mt. Eolus, one of the Needle Mountains. The year was 1927. Some forty years later, two miners would stake a claim on top of Mt. Eolus and name it *Day Breakers*, after the title of a L'Amour novel.

The nineteen-year-old adventurer watched bears through his binoculars and sometimes trailed them, but at a safe distance. He looked down and saw eagles soaring in the vast canyons below. He sat sipping coffee in the Bent Elbow in Silverton, his mind wondering what Columbine County had been like during the boom times, when Wyatt Earp and other Western figures dropped by, perhaps to sit and sip coffee and trade stories in Bent Elbow, too. Once L'Amour was taken for a horseback ride by the famous Buffalo Bill, who L'Amour recalled, "smelled slightly of bourbon and tobacco." Once when L'Amour cut hay in Lincoln, New Mexico, he worked beside two old-timers who had known Billy the Kid. A gangling, skinny adolescent, L'Amour would simply hang back and listen to the old-timers reminisce.

Later in life, L'Amour liked to hold forth on Billy the Kid when interviewed: "Billy the Kid? I imagine I can recollect as much about him as anybody now living," he told *Writer's Digest*. "I've talked with two women and five men who knew him personally. Good with cards. Good with a gun. Much maligned by writers today, who attempt to psychoanalyze him in print and pin a psychopath label on him. His problem was simply that when he got pushed, he pushed back, real hard."

In *Gun World* L'Amour reiterated that Billy the Kid was not the psychopath he'd been labelled. He simply got a bum rap, because of a notorious photograph taken after he had been holed-up sick in the mountains for weeks. When he came down, he was bundled up in far too many clothes, his hair was very long, and he appeared sick, which he was. In the photograph, the Kid looks wild or insane. Once he found himself rocking on a porch beside the Indian woman who had been given the task of preparing Billy the Kid's body for burial —a job he could relate to from his own funeral parlor days.

One of the five men who knew the Kid was George Coe, who L'Amour ran into during his knock-about days. Coe had been in the Lincoln County War with Billy, and lost a finger in a fight with Buckshot Roberts.

Another Western hero of L'Amour's was Jim Bowie, who he regarded as a genuine man of honor. "When he decided to battle for Texas independence, he rode six hundred miles just to tell Mexico's General

Santa Ana of his decision and why the two would have to fight. A magnificent gesture."

While L'Amour admired Billy the Kid and Jim Bowie, he appears to have had no use for Jesse James. This was based upon what he had heard and read. Before the Civil War, it seems, James had been both a horse thief and a murderer. L'Amour felt Hollywood always went astray when they portrayed Jesse James as a good guy who was merely misunderstood.

L'Amour's path actually crossed with Emmett Dalton, the last survivor of the Dalton gang. The others were wiped out in a botched attempt to hold up two banks at the same time in Coffeyville, Kansas. Emmett was badly wounded, but survived to spend fifteen years behind bars.

L'Amour found mining to be a dangerous and unexpected occupation. One night, shortly before one of his visits to Silverton, an entire lake dropped through a space approximately as long as two football fields. The ore body had simply been worked much too close to the bottom of the lake. Timber, tools, and boulders shot out of that tunnel as if propelled by a firehose. Sheriff Virgil Mason told the story to L'Amour when the young man returned to the area. L'Amour seems to have been lucky to have worked the mines so many times without personal injury.

He was good at survival. He knew better, for example, than to camp at the bottom of a canyon. There was too great a risk of a flash flood which could carry a man away. Rain that fell miles distant could, quite suddenly—and with no warning—come rushing through. When that happened, it was torrential and could last for minutes or hours. Rushing water could flood the canyon anywhere from a few feet high to thirty feet high.

During those mining days, L'Amour worked in hard-rock mines in the West— never, he claimed, in a coal mine—a fact which would make the circumstances of his death, years later, ironic. He worked silver, lead, zinc, and gold mines. In addition to tramming and shoveling, he was proud of his prowess with a doublejack—a sledge-hammer.

The best times for L'Amour were when the men broke for lunch or after work when the shift was done and there was downtime during which the miners counted their shots. This was when the old-timers told tales about the boom camps they had worked. L'Amour heard them recite all the magic names—Goldfield, Tonopah, Cripple Creek, Leadville, Rawhide, Virginia City. He listened to old outlaws retell how the Lincoln County wars took place. They recreated the personalities they had known, such as Shorty Harris, Ten-Day Murphy, and Slasher Harrington. Shorty Harris, it seems, was buried standing up at the bottom of Death Valley—the kind of detail a future writer would not forget.

Ever since his father had taught him how to box, the manly art had been a strong interest of L'Amour's. He encountered a tough old Irishman in one of the larger mines who had actually boxed a four-round exhibition with the great John L. Sullivan. Other miners L'Amour met had seen Joe Gans fight Battling Nelson for the world's lightweight title. After an amazing forty-two rounds, Gans won the match on a foul.

Later, at various places he passed through or where he worked, the youthful

L'Amour boxed eleven times—and outside the ring over twice that many times; being the new kid in town was never easy. He got $25 for his first fight. His biggest purse came many years later, in Singapore, when he won $1800 by a knockout in seven rounds. Eighteen hundred dollars was a tidy sum at that time. Once in Shanghai he would be pitted against a 250-pound Russian. L'Amour weighed about 175 at the time. But he won that match with a convincing belly punch!

L'Amour would use his boxing experiences as background for a series of private detective stories featuring a character named Kip Morgan. The character's mother named him after Rudyard Kipling, one of L'Amour's lifelong enthusiasms. Morgan is depicted as an ex-prizefighter who is attempting to begin a new life as a private detective. Kip's adventures give us some insight into the moral dilemmas L'Amour faced as a fighter: trying to stay honest in a world of dishonest people who are drawn to the ring. Like L'Amour, Morgan is a light heavyweight. And also like L'Amour, he gives up the ring but never gives up his competitive edge.

Among the Kip Morgan stories are "Dead Man's Trail," "With Death In His Corner," and "The Street of Lost Corpses," all collected in *The Hills of Homicide* (1983).

Throughout these knock-about years, when he actually was a hobo, the young L'Amour continued to read. He actually found that he could learn better outside of school rather than inside. "When I was asked by other kids about dropping out," he bragged, "I tell them they should drop out only if they have read from fifty to one hundred non-fiction books per year for three years, for fun."

Throughout his books there is praise for self-education. "You are your own best teacher," he wrote in *The Walking Drum*. "My advice is to question all things. Seek for answers, and when you find what seems to be an answer, question that, too." In *The Lonely Men* he wrote, "My books have been the mountains, the desert, the forest, and the wide places where the grass grows." From his novels and stories, it is clear that Louis L'Amour held the belief that a school is wherever a man can learn, be it a mountain or a forest or a stream. A man learns by seeing, listening, hearing other men talk.

He felt men had to be good listeners to be good learners. Then one thinks about what one has heard, and filters it into one's own experience. L'Amour's philosophy is especially apparent in *Bendigo Shafter*, which received the prestigious American Book Award in 1980.

The teenager's fascination with the frontier was boundless. As his character Jubal Sackett proclaims, "... my star hung up over the western mountains and I knew it." L'Amour was the kind of man who always ventures toward whatever it is that lies beyond, onward and westward. He had to blaze his own trail. In *Bendigo Shafter* he declares, "The promised land is always a distant land ... it is a land one never attains."

As an adult he would write about various aspects of the American frontier experience. This would include the courageous early settlers of the seventeenth century, down through the generations of builders and makers who followed in their steps across the North American continent.

Perhaps L'Amour's most extended musings on the frontier are contained in the book which he titled *Frontier*. Unlike other books by L'Amour, this one will not be found on the paperback rack at a truck stop. Rather, it is a large, glossy coffee table book or art box, with stunning color nature photographs by David Muench. The volume is a celebration of the American land, its history and geology, and it is L'Amour's only work of non-fiction published to date.

In over twenty-five essays, L'Amour personally guides the reader across the North American continent. His prose is filled with historical and geological facts. Despite his pronouncements about learning from the land, L'Amour always did his homework with reference books. In later life, his Bel Air California home was filled with over 10,000 books of history and fact. In fact, some accounts bring the total to 20,000 volumes. He, no doubt, recalled the distinct comfort in having that family library of three hundred books in North Dakota while he was growing up.

Published in 1984, *Frontier* is a verbal and visual reinforcement of the world of Louis L'Amour's imagination. It also is the closest account so far to an autobiography of L'Amour. In it, he tells of many of his experiences during his years of back-country traveling. He shares the singular sensations of going above the timberline to the places of eagles, of walking a desert mile, and of the unusual beauty of the bayous. His theory of why people opened up the country is distilled quite simply as this: While they found excuses for going—to trap for fur, to pan for gold—the real reason was always that they wished to extend their own horizons, to look for a better life. In this way, his father's move from the Dakotas to Oklahoma was repeating the pattern of his frontier forebears, and Louis' New Mexico travels were yet another expression of this search for new opportunities.

Some reviewers and writers, assessing L'Amour's work, express surprise in the relatively infrequent appearance of bloodshed and badmen. Yet in *Frontier*, L'Amour pointedly reminds us: "The lawlessness in Western communities has been much overrated because of its dramatic aspects. The stories of outlaws and badmen are exciting, and Western men themselves still love to relate them. However, over most of the

West schools and churches had come with the first settlers, and law accompanied them. The gunfighters and cardsharks were on the wrong side of the tracks, most of them unknown to the general run of the population, although they might be pointed out on occasion."

L'Amour's books are relatively free of violence when compared to most Westerns, despite some gun play and instances of hanging, torture and cannibalism. This is intentional. He felt gunfights were greatly overplayed in most genre novels. He was fond of reminding interviewers that, between 1800 and 1816, "there were as many gunfights in our Navy as on the entire frontier." And he felt there was much more happening in the frontier than just gunfights and Indian battles. He was interested more in the meeting of cultures and counter influences.

While he downplayed the gratuitous violence of gunslingers and hired killers, Louis L'Amour's typical fictional hero, however, was no pushover. Far from it. As he explained to C. Gerald Fraser in an interview for the *New York Times*, "when you open a rough, hard country like that, it's a rough, hard, bitter life and you don't open it with a lot of pantywaists." He went on: "The men who came West were . . . the pick of the country. They were physically and psychologically tough." In *The Hills of Homicide*, he wrote, "when somebody tries to make it with a gun, he has already admitted he hasn't the guts to make it the honest way. Whether he realizes it or not, life has already whipped him. From there on in, it's all downhill."

"People are upset about violence," he told Hank Nuwer. "It's because they don't understand violence. There's always been violence in the world. This is one thing people forget. Every creative period has been a time of great turmoil. In the Renaissance, for example, people were being murdered on the streets every night. You hardly dared walk out on the street at certain hours without a bodyguard around you. Every creative period is this way because it's the only expression that many people have. Everyone is trying to express himself. He feels something is happening. The world is bursting apart around him, and he wants to be part of it—subconsciously at least."

No doubt the heroes of his novels resembled an older version of the strapping fifteen-year-old who left Jamestown to find himself in the backcountry. The many young male L'Amour protagonists not only have a deep respect for nature and the land, but an admiration for the Indians as well. They also are often depicted as having a great respect for learning. Bendigo Shafter reads Montaigne's *Essays*, and Drake Morrell reads Juvenal's *Satires*—in Latin!

By 1926, the land no longer held a sufficient challenge for the youthful L'Amour. He set his sights on the sea. He rode freight trains from El Paso to the Gulf of Mexico, where he first went to sea at the age of seventeen. He travelled to the West Indies where he claimed to have been shipwrecked and even to Europe.

Later, he worked his way to San Pedro, California. Still in his teens, he had reached his full height, and the years of hard work had given him a mature look. He was able to pass himself off as a twenty-two-year-old man when he went to what was then called the Marine Service Bureau. Seamen called the Bureau "Fink Hall" or, worse, "The

Slave Market". L'Amour registered with the Bureau as seaman but had to wait his turn to be taken on as a crewmember of a ship—a wait which could last as long as three months.

During this time, he lived in an on-shore dormitory run by the Seaman's Institute. It provided him the use of a reading room, game room, and a mailing address. The checker playing he witnessed in the game room was some of the best and most competitive, he had ever seen. One man he met in San Pedro became the protagonist for L'Amour's later story, "Survival," and he and L'Amour were to ship-out as bunkmates.

Times in San Pedro were hard. For every job, there were ten men. About all the out-of-towners waiting for ships could get to do was paint or buck rivets in the shipyard, swamp on a truck, or take an occasional "stand-by" job on a ship. L'Amour and the other men often went without meals. Having obtained his seaman's papers, L'Amour sometimes went aboard steam schooners like the *Yellowstone*, the *Humboldt*, and the *Catherine G. Sudden* looking for work. While there, he would beg a meal.

Waiting around wasn't L'Amour's style, and when he finally did leave San Pedro, it was by taking what the old wind-ship sailors used to call a "pierhead jump". One night he was at the Seaman's Institute, checking the lists to see what ships were due to arrive and what their destinations would be, though the latter hardly mattered to him—he would sail anywhere. According to a biographical sketch in his story collection, *Yondering*, on this particular evening he had exactly five cents in his pocket. None of the regulars were around when a stranger came in, looking for an extra seaman. "You're lucky," L'Amour replied. He carried the man's sea bag to the ship, since he had nothing of his own to carry. L'Amour would have to buy his outfit from the ship's slop closet.

As it turned out, the ship was a freighter bound for the Far East. L'Amour signed on in the chief mate's cabin. He had no idea what he was getting into. He was broke, and it was a job. It couldn't be worse than skinning nine hundred and twenty-five dead and rotting cattle. He couldn't foresee he'd soon be fighting off pirates in Indonesia.

The ship became his home for the next six

months. He became ship's watchman. The ship was bound for Liverpool, England. The philosophical young swabby said, "Everything loose eventually washed down to the sea." He traveled to Yokohama, Kobe, Nagasaki, Shanghai (where he celebrated his eighteenth birthday), and Hong Kong, as well as ports in Borneo, Java, Sumatra, Singapore, and the Malay States. He told of fighting off pirates who invaded his ship from some offshore Malay island. His only weapon was a broken oar with a splintered end, which he brandished as a pitchfork. Of that encounter he spoke, "You don't think about the danger . . . You don't have the time. And you don't have time to get scared until afterwards, either. Fear always comes later . . ." He jumped ship in China, according to some accounts, where he ended up in the badlands, "where no white man lived." In any event, he did knock about the Far East and he later related the horror of seeing criminals beheaded in China.

Next, he returned to Shanghai, where he came to know and be known by the patrons of the Astor Bar and the lesser-known International Bar. Both were frequented by soldiers and sailors of fortune who sold their skills to war lords wherever there was a conflict. One-Arm Sutton and General Frederick Townsend Ward were two legends L'Amour encountered there. Sutton had been employed by a half-dozen war lords in China, building mortars. An accident resulted in the loss of a limb.

It was One-Arm Sutton who first told L'Amour about Siberia in great detail. Sutton had gone from his native Canada to Siberia in an attempt to steal some gold bars the White Russian Army had stored there. He also dredged for gold. His accounts of the forbidding frontier captured L'Amour's imagination. He wrote several stories set in Siberia, the first of which was "Wings Over Khabarovsk," which he included in *Night Over the Solomons*. And of course, Siberia would be the setting for his novel, *Last of the Breed* (1986).

If L'Amour is to be believed, his adventures included fighting for Chiang Kai-shek and living with a group of bandits in the mountains of Western China and Tibet for ten months. He later told his daughter, Angelique, about walking through the Tibetan mountains. The trail narrowed to a space only three inches wide, with a drop of a couple hundred feet on one side. He wondered at the time just what in hell he was doing up there!

During these years, his penchant for getting involved in brawls continued. There was one big one in Shanghai, when the crews of two destroyers, a cruiser, and a couple of freighters "took on almost half the British navy." The following night, ironically, they were all drinking together and being buddies. Another brawl he reports having missed: He and a Dutch second-cook from his ship were in a fish and chip shop in Liverpool, with a couple of girls, when four enormous Norwegians came in looking for a fight. But the cook "whipped all four of them before I could get the girl off my lap," he told Harold Keith.

L'Amour also reports he spent a year in India, crossing the country on a bicycle, following the route of Rudyard Kipling's Kim. He is said to have traveled from Afghanistan to Iran with a camel caravan, and become a tourist guide in Egypt after having only been there for eight hours.

All of this may in fact be true, but there are times, given such tales, when L'Amour's fiction-telling abilities might also extend to aspects of his own life. If so, his autobiography, when published, may contain some of his best fiction.

This should not be a surprise. Writers have always known that there is no such thing as telling only the truth. As author Larry Woiwode has said, "Every autobiography is fiction. We know that memory is absolutely inaccurate. I think the older we grow, the more we know that memory lies; we might even say that when a person tries most to be autobiographical he or she lies the most."[3]

Whether or not his accounts can entirely be trusted, there is no question that L'Amour crammed more into these few years than most men experience in a lifetime. Not even Ernest Hemingway had a more adventurous young manhood.

Take, for instance, L'Amour's adventure in Macao, where he had the first great stroke of luck in his life. In a bar, L'Amour happened to overhear some men making elaborate plans to recover money from a sunken ship. They talked as if it were a

3. *New York Times*, Sept. 5, 1988

great sum of money, but did not specify how much. L'Amour went into action. He acquired diving gear and somehow located the ship. He beat the men to that sunken treasure, and when he counted it, it turned out to be $50,000.

Laughing all the way, the young man used the money to take him to Paris, where he attempted to lead the Bohemian life. That sort of life ultimately did not agree with him. From Paris, he bicycled to Marseilles, and later went to Italy and Hungary. He says he returned to America only after all the money ran out. This makes a fine story. But in the autobiographical sketch he wrote for *Yondering*, L'Amour states he remained on the ship he boarded in San Pedro: "With stops here and there we went around the world to finally pay off in Brooklyn."

From New York, he next took a tanker and went around to the West Coast via the Panama Canal. On his first long trip he had served as an ordinary seaman. But on his third voyage he asked for, and passed, an examination that promoted him to able-bodied seaman. The pay was better. Yet another adventure had him shipping on a schooner as second mate. One of his many duties was to account for everything bought and sold by his bright but near-illiterate captain.

As he wandered from port to port, L'Amour met adventurers, pirates, planters, pearl buyers, and gold seekers—men like himself who were wandering the ends of the earth. They were not, he admitted to himself, unlike the men he had been acquainted with back on the ranches and in the mines. But somehow they had different motivations. Frontier men desired to build something out of nothing. These men just wanted to get rich quick.

The ships L'Amour sailed around the East Indian islands had the capability to get inside small ports which the large steamships and freighters had to avoid. In a launch with an outboard motor, the young man could visit remote places others could not. One result of these adventures was a series of stories with a hero named Ponga Jim Mayo. Ponga Jim is a sailor of fortune and the master of a tramp freighter. He sailed out of Liverpool to the west coast of the Ponga River in Africa, hence his nickname.

L'Amour thrived on the gossip, intrigue, and inherent danger which existed in harbors, waterfront bars, and ports of call. In 1986, he wrote that he almost wished he were back on the waterfronts again; he missed the smells of the sea, the tar, and the rotting fruit. He loved those end-of-the-world ports like Amurang, Port Moresby, Broome, Hollandia, and Gorontalo. And he was fascinated that so many of the ports had not changed throughout the years. Once he hired an Arab boy to sail him to a nearby island. It had an old ruin he wanted to explore. The boy spoke English, so L'Amour asked him in passing just how long the boy had been on the islands. He replied that his people had lived there for almost four centuries!

One unrealized dream from this period in L'Amour's life was his plan to found an express-passenger air operation in what is now Indonesia. With a friend who was a bush pilot, and had already been flying planters and prospectors into the Amazon-Orinoco country, L'Amour planned to get rich, flying people who were willing to pay outrageous sums to get in and out of places inaccessible by boat. But he dropped the scheme when his stories began to be bought by the pulps back in the States.

The notion of tramp piloting never left him. It resulted in the character of Turk Madden, who flies for a living in some stories in *Night Over the Solomons*.

In that book, L'Amour recalls observing Germans and Japanese preparing for World War II, depositing large amounts of equipment on the islands. He had heard about pocket submarines while in the East Indies two years before they first appeared at Pearl Harbor. He could feel war in the air. One time, prior to the outbreak of hostilities, his small ship overcame a large German freighter. One German defected and hid on L'Amour's ship, in exchange for work; the ship was short-handed. When the Germans came looking for the defector, L'Amour and the others hid him in the shaft alley, where he went undetected. The ship captain had to go ashore more than once to speak to the German consul. But the stowaway remained on board when they left port. He was never detected.

L'Amour was very canny. In the title story of *Night Over the Solomons*, he wrote of a Japanese base on the island of Kolombangara. No one had ever told him there was, in fact, a base there. He merely had looked at a map and figured that, if the U.S. had troops fighting on Guadacanal, the Japanese would be wise to have a base on Kolombangara in order to cut off American supplies. Shortly after the story was published stateside, the Navy discovered an actual Japanese base on the island. L'Amour never took credit for that event. He wrote that he doubted if the magazine in which his story appeared had ever reached the South Pacific by the time of the discovery.

While L'Amour continued to submit stories to magazines back in the States, much of what he wrote during these years —poetry as well as fiction—was lost, either due to the mails, or his continual moving around.

However, much of his accounts of these adventures is true, L'Amour's travels abroad surely taught him the need for tolerance if one is to survive in this world, even when others are intolerant. At the same time, he learned to be wary of men. This is reflected in *The Lonesome Gods*.

CHAPTER THREE

FAME

When Louis L'Amour returned to the United States in 1939, he was thirty-one years old. He made his way to Oklahoma City, where he was reunited with his parents. They lived on acreage in the nearby town of Choctaw. It was a joyous time for the LaMoores, seeing their son again, and hearing the richness of the stories he related of his exotic adventures.

He lived with his parents in Choctaw for several months. During this time, he started writing stories and poems, knocking them out on an old, beat-up Underwood manual typewriter. He began to mine the files of small-town newspapers, looking for stories. The early tales he wrote were not Westerns. Rather, they were gangster, boxing, and adventure tales. He submitted some to the pulp magazines, of which he has written:

"My stories came back like homing pigeons ... I had more than 200 rejection slips ... Frankly," he told Hank Nuwer, "that's when my training as a fighter helped me ... One thing you learn early is that if you get knocked down, you've got to get up again. It's the same thing with writing." He realized that he had to be less wordy, more direct, and to the point. L'Amour decided to study the work of his favorite writers, to determine what he was doing wrong. He re-read stories by Robert Louis Stevenson, O. Henry, de Maupassant, and Jack London. These, and half a dozen stories from current magazines, became his models.

"What I learned is that you have to start telling the story from the very first line."

He realized he had been doing what every novice writer does, "talking about the story for three pages before I ever started writing." Another trick he learned was to start the story in the middle of the action, not at the beginning or close to the end. Then the use of flashbacks would fill in all the gaps.

After a while, he got the knack. His first sale was for the grand sum of $6.50, to magazine entitled *True Gang Life*. It was a short-short story about a gang killing. A witness against a gangster is killed by a hit-man. But the dead witness turns out to be the gangster's own brother whom he had been sending to school. The twist in plot and the compassion between the brothers would prefigure some of the work of the mature L'Amour.

Another story fetched $40, and it wasn't long before he was writing novellas and selling them for up to $600—which in 1939 was a considerable sum. It could, for example, buy a new car. In the foreword to *West from Singapore*, L'Amour reports that he was writing a novel at this time. But it was never completed because he was drafted for the armed services.

During these months in Choctaw, he became friendly with some of the writing professors and students at the University of Oklahoma in Norman. He never matriculated, as has sometimes been reported, but nevertheless he absorbed what he could. Among his friends on the Norman campus were Dr. Walter Campbell and Foster Harris, both part of the university's writing program. L'Amour was later to proclaim that it was by "far the best and I've seen lots of them." Other friends at O.U. included Dr. Carl Coke Ritter and Dr. E.E. Dale, both historians of the Southwest and specialists in American Natives; Dr. Joseph Brandt, then director of the university press and later the university's president; Ben Botkin, Elgin Groseclose, Dr. Paul B. Sears, Dr. Savoie Lottinville, and Dr. Kenneth Kaufman.

It was Dr. Kaufman who had the greatest influence on L'Amour. He edited the book review page for the *Oklahoman* in Oklahoma City. L'Amour received an advance copy of *Anthony Adverse*, wrote a favorable review predicting the novel would be a great success, and submitted it to Kaufman. The review was accepted, and Kaufman began to send L'Amour other books to review for the paper. He invited him to visit him in his home town of Norman as well, and that led to a friendship that L'Amour greatly valued. Kaufman was not only a professor and an editor, he was also a poet. He gave his new friend a copy of his own poetry volume, *Level Land*. He inscribed it,

TO LOUIS L'AMOUR, WHO WILL BE
HEARD FROM SOME DAY.

Little did Kaufman know how well-known L'Amour would become—not as a poet, but as a novelist.

By L'Amour's count, he was reviewing from two to five books a week for the Sunday *Oklahoman*. He was also writing poetry, some of it quite formal. In fact, when his first book was accepted for publication, it was not fiction at all, but a collection of these rather florid poems. Entitled, *Smoke From This Altar*, it was published perhaps at L'Amour's own expense by a small firm, Lusk Publishing Company, located in Oklahoma City. The young man was proud to have tangible evidence that he was, in fact, a published author.

The book was not much: Three dozen, mostly brief poems, about violent nature and a protagonist who constantly hears the call of the wild. To L'Amour's credit, fifteen of the poems are Italian sonnets.

At this point in his life, L'Amour returned to prize fighting—an extremely curious occupation for a poet—but he needed the money. Boxing as a light heavy-weight, he was quite successful. He won all but five of his 59 fights. Some reference versions say the number was 51, still other accounts set it at 54. Thirty-four were won by knock-out.

"I never lost a fight when I was eating regularly," he once said. In addition to fighting, he coached a Golden Gloves boxing team at Choctaw. That was a mixed experience. It taught him, he confessed, that it was easier to take a beating yourself, than to see some kid you had trained, take one.

Then he abruptly left Choctaw and returned to New York City. The start of World War II was imminent. The date of publication of his book of poetry in 1939 coincided with Adolf Hitler's invasion of Poland. Great Britain and France had declared war. Eventually, Japan's air raid attack on Pearl Harbor on December 7, 1941, would pull the U.S. into the war against not only Japan, but Germany and Italy, as well. According to his sister, L'Amour did not want to enter the military; he was afraid it would interrupt his writing career.

Before the start of World War II, and just after its beginnings, he was writing the stories that later were published in *Night Over the Solomons* and *West from Singapore*. He wrote in a foreword to a reprint of the latter that these stories were a frantic attempt to put food on the table while he was working on a novel.

The stories he was writing at this time were not of the West at all, but of the sea. L'Amour was hooked on the Pacific Islands as well as the area included in the Southeast Asian coasts. Their color, their excitement, fascinated him. It is interesting to note that the Dean of Westerns first learned his craft as the author of stories about the Indonesian islands.

Prior to the invasion of Europe, L'Amour journeyed to the United Kingdom and explored the English countryside, the lowlands and coastal areas. He also roamed the cities. Later he would make good use of all this background as origins for the fictitious families of his various sagas.

Finally, in 1942, L'Amour was drafted. At first he had been told he would be put in naval intelligence, where his knowledge of both the Far East and Eastern languages could be of use. Instead, he found himself a buck private dressed in olive drab. First he taught winter-survival techniques in Michigan. He served two years stateside. Then he was shipped overseas and stationed in France, where he was in the tank-destroyer and transportation corps for another two years. He served in Patton's Third Army during the march on Paris, and was with the Ninth Army at the crossing of the Ruhr. He rose to the rank of First Lieutenant.

During the war, to pass the time, he told his fellow Yanks some of the stories he had had told to him during his wandering/ yondering years. They had heard nothing to match them, and encouraged him to write down more of these stories. Contrary to his earlier fears, the war did not interrupt his writing. He wrote extensively while serving his country, and in the late 1940s these stories finally began to appear in such pulps as *Detective Tales*, *G-Men Detective*, *Popular Sports*, *Thrilling Adventures*, and *Sky Fighter*. He also wrote and published some Western stories at this time, but didn't think too much about them. Some of these stories were published in such magazines as *Giant Western*, *Popular Western*, *Thrilling Western*, and *Rio Kid Western*.

L'Amour was a good soldier. He knew how to read terrain which was essential to his assignment of duty. He knew that much of any confrontation depends upon the terrain and how a soldier uses it to his advantage. Yet, fighting was a craft he had to learn like mining and sonnet-writing. As he wrote in *Lando*, "Until you know how to fight with your head as well as with your heart and muscle, you are no fighting man."

L'Amour fought with his head. He was even able to think of war in poetic terms, as did the young Stephen Crane—author of *The Red Badge of Courage*—before him. "Yet when a man walks out with weapons," L'Amour was to write in *Jubal Sackett*, "his life is suspended like dew upon a spider's web."

During his years in the service, one published report stated that L'Amour was awarded four bronze stars. He served as a range officer. Once a soldier complained that his M-1 rifle could not be zeroed in properly. "Let me see it," L'Amour said casually. He then reported that, "offhand from five hundred yards," he shot "twenty-nine consecutive bullseyes." He went on in *Gun World* to describe the feat: "Obviously, I was not under any pressure, merely trying to check out the soldier's complaint. But as I kept hitting the black, a crowd began to grow around me. The hoopla was getting louder with each shot and the pressure not to miss was keeping apace. After the twenty-ninth squeeze, I quit while I was ahead."

In *Writer's Digest*, Arthur F. Gonzalez Jr. has L'Amour commanding a platoon of the "Red Ball Express," the legendary unit of oil tankers that accompanied General Patton's armour, bringing up the fuel the cavalry brigades consumed. Whether or not L'Amour participated in the D-Day landings is in dispute. His sister, Mrs. Edna LaMoore Waldo, says categorically in her unpublished handwritten memoirs that he did not. But an article in *Roundup* published in December, 1954, states that he "was in every major action from D-Day on except the Battle of the Bulge." It is possible that in interviews L'Amour intensified his participation, just as the number of cattle he skinned and prize fights he won kept increasing through the years.

In 1946, he received an honorable discharge. He returned first to New York City, and one of the earliest phone calls he made was to Leo Margulies. Margulies was an editor at the office of *Thrilling Adventures*, among forty-seven other magazines! It was Margulies who had bought L'Amour's second published story. During the course of their phone conversation, the editor invited L'Amour to a party. It proved to be one of the most important nights of the author's life. During the party Margulies asked L'Amour what he planned on doing, now that he was out of the service. L'Amour replied that he really didn't know but that he was going to somehow have to make a living. The editor thought, then said, "Look —I know you know about the West. I've talked to you about it. So why don't you write me some Western stories?"

L'Amour did, submitted them, and they were bought. He needed quick money, and the pulps paid in ten to fourteen days. Soon he was selling more Western stories than any other kind. These stories were published under the names "Tex Burns" and also "Jim May," a name L'Amour took from the Ponga Jim Mayo stories he had written sometime earlier.

Not all his writing went to the pulps. *Colliers* magazine began to buy his work. He later expanded one such story at the suggestion of the magazine into a novel. Eventually the manuscript would become L'Amour's classic western, *Hondo*.

L'Amour made another major decision in 1946. He moved to Los Angeles, where he felt he could be at the center of the Western industry. At least Western films, serials and the like, were being produced there. Later, of course, Western television series would also be produced there. Louis L'Amour would be heavily represented in both media.

There is a widespread notion that L'Amour wrote only Westerns after his move to the West Coast. The fact is, he continued to write hardboiled detective stories from 1946 until sometime in the 1950s. Eight were collected in 1983 in *The Hills of Homicide*, under circumstances which will be expanded upon later. But it is clear, that most of his output from this time forward, was Westerns. Eventually, he progressed toward the longer form and completed a novel. Entitled, *Westward the Tide*, the novel was published first in London by World Works. Like Robert Frost, Louis L'Amour appeared first in book form in the United Kingdom. This is contrary to two errors which have been perpetuated through the years. The first is that *Hondo* was L'Amour's first novel. This error has been printed in a number of Bantam editions of his novels. The second is that *Hopalong Cassidy and the Rustlers of West Fork* was his initial novel. That work's first appearance was in *Hopalong Cassidy's Western Magazine*, also in 1950, as the lead novel in the premier issue. It was published in book form by Doubleday, later the same year. Both versions were issued under the pseudonym Tex Burns.

Between 1950 and 1952, L'Amour published four Hopalong Cassidy books, all with Doubleday, and all under the Tex Burns moniker. The second, *Hopalong Cassidy and the Trail to Seven Pines*, appeared in 1951 in the second, and final, issue of the Cassidy magazine before appearing as a book.

This was really hack writing for L'Amour. He not only had to be true to the original characters as developed by Hopalong creator, Clarence E. Mulford, but he also somehow had to make the characters adhere to the characterization of the actors who portrayed them in the popular movies which starred William "Hopalong" Boyd. This experience had the virtue of giving L'Amour practice in plotting.

Once he took up residence in Hollywood, L'Amour began to write and be published steadily. His career was never to be the same once he published the story, "The Gift of Cochise," in *Colliers* on July 5th, 1952. It proved to be one of his best and most admired stories. And the editor's casual suggestion that he expand it into a novel led to his second great stroke of luck. But, as with many people, L'Amour made his own good luck. It didn't just befall him. How L'Amour came to get the expanded story published, now in novel form and known as *Hondo*, is a study in confidence and perhaps a little gall.

Saul David was editorial director of a large paperback publishing house in New York City in the 1950s. The firm had lost their star Western writer, Luke Short. David packed his bags and visited Hollywood, hoping to scout some new talent. While there, he stayed at the posh pink palace, the Beverly Hills Hotel. Word was out that the editor was in town.

One day the telephone in David's hotel room rang. It was Louis L'Amour calling. He told David that he might not yet have heard of him, but he was going to be the next Luke Short, or bigger. Probably bigger. He asked David to see him immediately. The editor invited the stranger to come up.

When L'Amour arrived at his room, he had a big envelope of his writing under his arm. He thrust it at David, and then sat and watched the man's reactions as he read. What David read was sample chapters of *Hondo*. The manuscript totally engrossed him. He signed L'Amour on the spot to a long-term contract.

In *Smithsonian* magazine, thirty-four years later, L'Amour recounted that Saul David was with Bantam Books at the time. However, it was Fawcett Books who publised *Hondo* in 1953 under its imprint, a Gold Medal Book. L'Amour's contract with Bantam was to come later. Fawcett put all their considerable promotional skills behind the novel. Not only were some 320,000 copies of *Hondo* initially printed and sold, but Fawcett also managed to sell the film rights—for a surprisingly low price of $4,000, considering John Wayne was both behind the filming and its star. While L'Amour never used a literary agent, he did later acquire an agent named Mauri Grashin for his movie deals.

The *Hondo* paperback was promoted by two-color truck posters, counter cards, and dealer promotions. The book and the movie version were released simultaneously, on November 25, 1953, the day the film opened in New York City. On that day, the Gold Medal paperback was on newsstands all over America. L'Amour's father did not live to see his son's enormous success. He died in 1952. But L'Amour's proud mother saw it all.

This was not a novelization of a film script of *Hondo*. It was the publication of a new and original novel and the film based on it, both released on the same day—an unusual event, even now. The novel was to become L'Amour's most popular work; by 1980, it had sold over three million copies. According to L'Amour, it was used in college writing classes.

Directed by James Edward Grant, and produced by Robert Fellows, the movie, filmed in the then popular 3-D process, was helped enormously by inspired casting. It featured John Wayne as "Hondo Lane," the scout and dispatch rider, and the great Geraldine Page as "Angie Lowe." Page was nominated for an Academy Award for Best Actress for her performance. Wayne had great enthusiasm for this project. He called *Hondo* "the best Western novel I ever read," and allowed that blurb to be printed on the book's cover, where it remains today.

Conversely, L'Amour was equally enthusiastic about the film version. In a number of later interviews he proclaimed it, "the best movie made from my work."

In a conversation with Michael T. Marsden he elaborated, "it was an exceptionally well-done picture. I wanted a girl ... who looked like she had been living out in the desert for quite a while, and Geraldine Page didn't mind a bit. And Wayne, of course, was the typical Western man. He really was. They played it beautifully in the situation. The desert was right, the Indians were right, everything was right."

In that same conversation, L'Amour expanded on his intentions in *Hondo*: "What I was telling there was the story of three people living their lives against an Indian outbreak in the background. An Indian chief was leading his people in a battle he knew he couldn't win. A man who is fiercely independent, even to the extent that the dog along with him is not his dog; he's his own dog. A woman who had a home and who was going to cling to it regardless of everything else, it was her whole being. She had a son at home and even though it was dangerous to stay there, she was going to try and stay ..."

On the basis of *Hondo*, L'Amour was signed to a one-book-a-year contract with Fawcett. That same year, 1953, he brought out *Showdown at Yellow Butte*, and in 1954, *Utah Blaine*, which—in view of the enormous publicity for *Hondo*—was curiously published under the pen-name "Jim Mayo."

Why L'Amour gave in to editorial demands is uncertain. Once again, he was told by an editor at *Standard* magazines that there was doubt that the public would purchase Westerns written by someone named L'Amour. Readers wanted something more Western-sounding—whatever that was. So L'Amour rummaged among his characters' names and once more came up with "Jim Mayo."

The same year that *Utah Blaine* was published, L'Amour's mother died. Now he was in real life parentless, as are so many of the young heroes in his novels. Strangely, both brothers Parker and Bill also died in 1954. It was, emotionally, a tough year. He had never taken a wife, so he was now totally without immediate family. Soon, however, he was sufficiently famous to abandon all pen-names. When *Utah Blaine* was made into a film in 1958, it was acknowledged as a Louis L'Amour property.

He signed a contract with Bantam Books

in 1955 which stipulated two books a year. This was later changed to the highly ambitious agreement for three books a year—a prospect which daunted L'Amour not at all. By that time he already had published, since *Hondo*, *Showdown at Yellow Butte* (1953), *Crossfire Trail* (1954), *Kilkenny* (1954), *Utah Blaine* (1954), *Guns of the Timberlands* (1955), *Heller with a Gun* (1955), and *To Tame a Land* (1955). Obviously he was producing at least three books a year; he may as well be guaranteed to get paid for them.

The year 1955 saw production of two more films based on his work: *Treasure of Ruby Hills* (Allied Artists), directed by Frank McDonald, and based on the short story "Riders of the Ruby Hills"; and *Stranger on Horseback* (United Artists), directed by Jacques Tourneur.

In 1956 he produced two more novels— *Silver Canyon* (published first in England by Bouregy & Curl), and *The Burning Hills*. The latter would be serialized in *The Saturday Evening Post* and made into a Warner Brothers movie the same year, with a script by another world-wide best-selling author, Irving Wallace. The film starred Tab

Hunter and Natalie Wood, and the wonderful character actor, Skip Homeier, who had been so menacing in the 1950 Western classic, *The Gunfighter*, starring Gregory Peck in an atypical role.

But the biggest news of 1956 was that Louis L'Amour got married, for the first and only time. The man who so advocated family and the hearth in his books was finally creating a family of his own.

CHAPTER FOUR

FAMILY

The scene was The Grand Ballroom of the Los Angeles Beverly Hilton Hotel, a glittering space so unlike the settings of his novels. It was there, on February 19, 1956, that Louis L'Amour took Katherine ("Kathy") Elizabeth Adams to be his bride. The couple took an extended honeymoon in the West Indies and South America's northern coast.

Katherine Adams was not the first romantic interest in L'Amour's life. In past inter-

views, he had revealed earlier relation-
ships. He said he once was engaged to a
French countess who was a widow with two
children. The affair did not work out, pri-
marily because of the difference in their
lifestyles. After that, the handsome bachelor dated a number of women. His age
seemed to demand that they be starlets. He
then became engaged to the actress, Julie
Newmar. And it was Ms. Newmar who introduced L'Amour to the very pretty bru-
nette, Kathy Adams.

At the time of their marriage, Kathy
L'Amour was only twenty-two years old.
Louis L'Amour was forty-eight, making
theirs a real May-December marriage. It
was the first marriage for each. The
daughter of a real-estate developer, Kathy's
forebears had come from England and
Scotland. She had attended Westlake
School for Girls, and later went to U.C.L.A.
She had lived in and around Hollywood for
years, became friends with Julie Newmar,
and pursued an acting career. Her roles
included parts on such television series as
"Death Valley Days" and "Gunsmoke".
Kathy obviously could relate to western

culture and drama much better than the French countess!

When they wed, L'Amour's career as a very well-paid author was clearly established. His new wife, on the other hand, was a starlet and not yet a name actress. She willingly abandoned her career plans to become Mrs. Louis L'Amour. That they remained married for thirty-two years—to the day he died—is testimony to the solidity of the match. Speaking of the marriage, he proclaimed, "That . . . is when I *really* struck it rich!" Elsewhere he said, "She's the perfect wife . . . In nineteen years I haven't found one thing I'd change or want other than it is. She is beautiful (acknowledged so by everyone), intelligent, reads a lot and is always busy with needlework and quilting."

If the last remark sounds a tad sexist, L'Amour went on to praise Kathy's sharp business mind and the fact that she was supervising the construction of a wing for him to work in at home. So he valued her mind as well as her needlework. Kathy helped make his life of full-time writer possible. She prepared his taxes, answered much of his mail, and arranged his many speaking engagements, which covered the globe.

Why had L'Amour not married until he was forty-eight? He told one reporter he had seen too many writers take inappropriate jobs that interfered with their writing, in order to support a family.

His thoughts on the subject of marriage may well have been in accord with what he wrote in *Bendigo Shafter:* "A wife and family don't get along with dreams. They hamper a man's movements. They restrict the risks he can afford to take to get ahead, and even the most helpful of women is usually more expense than a very young man can bear."

By the time he proposed to his wife-to-be, Louis L'Amour had realized his dream to be a writer. He could well afford the expense.

But expense was not the only consideration. During all his yondering years, L'Amour seemed to prefer solitude to companionship—either male or female. His goal seemed to be to see all he could see, and not just to see it, but to totally absorb it. Companionship was a detriment, a belief he expressed in several novels, but no where better than in *Jubal Sackett*: "A man who travels with another is only half as watchful as when traveling alone, and often less than half, for a part of his attention is diverted by his companion."

As for women, L'Amour seems to have appreciated the fair sex and wanted them, but not necessarily to have needed them. His reading of nature went deeper than his reading of the opposite sex. Even in *The Walking Drum*, a book he was to write years after being married, he wrote, "The deep sea can be fathomed, but who knows the heart of a woman?"

Perhaps L'Amour remained single so long because he knew he was a drifter at heart. A woman usually feels the need to find a man with roots, a man who belongs to one place providing a roof over them both, and their children to come.

A bit of cynicism toward women is found in his fiction as well. In *The Walking Drum*, again, he states that for a man to survive, all he need know is two sentences. The first is how to ask for food, and the second is how to tell a woman he loves her. Of the two, he regarded the second as the more important—because if you tell a woman you love her, she will certainly feed you!

But perhaps the truest statement of L'Amour's regard for women is found in *Sky-Liners*:

"... it runs in the blood of a man that he should care for womenfolk. It's a need in him, deep as motherhood to a woman and it's a thing folks are likely to forget ... If he's to feel of any purpose to himself, he's got to feel he's needed, feel he stands between somebody and any trouble."

It was decades before L'Amour stood between somebody.

The marriage produced two handsome children, a son, Beau Dearborn L'Amour, born in 1961, five years after the marriage, and a daughter, Angelique Gabrielle L'Amour, born three years later, in 1964. Both children have expressed interest in having careers as entertainers. Angelique has followed in the footsteps of both parents. Like her mother, she is an actress and a singer. And like her father, she confesses to a lifelong love of reading and writing.

Both children spent summers in Colorado with their parents, and Angelique helped her father with the extensive research for his books. She studied journalism at the University of Southern California, and it was she who compiled *A Trail of Memories: The Quotations of Louis L'Amour*, published in 1988.

In the introduction to that book, Louis L'Amour's daughter discusses a bit of what family life was like in Beverly Hills. Every morning until she went away to college, she would join her older brother and mother and father at the breakfast table. Then her father would read to the three of them. It was, the daughter admits, "a wonderful time of day."

Most of the books from which L'Amour read were related to the research he was conducting for his latest Western. But he also dipped into other areas—history, biography, even the naval adventure novels concerning H.M.S. Hornblower. And once in a great while, he would read from his own books: "This didn't happen too often, maybe six or seven times as I grew up," Angelique says. And the young girl found that to be the most magic reading of all. This makes sense, since L'Amour always professed to write to be read aloud.

"I'm a storyteller in the old folk tradition, like the man on a corner in the marketplace," he once remarked. Sometimes he compared himself to Chaucer. In an interview with *Writer's Digest*, he explained, "I really mean for my stories to be read aloud ... That's how I edit them. If it doesn't sound right to the ear, if it doesn't come out the way a ranch hand might say it, with a pipe in one hand and a cup of coffee in the other, then I change it."

The notion of L'Amour holding forth on editing himself may make some academics bristle. It is a known fact that he never revised a manuscript except for a few obvious grammatical or syntactical errors. He told *DLB Yearbook* that his first draft is always his last. His inconsistencies and repetitions, his violations of parallelism and poor punctuation, his split infinitives and generalized descriptions have all driven more than one critic to distraction. If L'Amour could not or would not clean up his manuscripts, where were his editors at Fawcett and Bantam?

It would appear that Bantam's Western editor, Irwyn Applebaum, developed a hands-off attitude toward L'Amour's manuscripts. While admitting, "You may find writers who produce a better book in terms of quality," Applebaum concluded, "but I don't think you'll ever find a better storyteller." This may well be true—but a story is told better when the point of view doesn't mysteriously switch from the first-person to the third, as it does at the conclusion of *Lonely on the Mountain*, for no apparent reason. "No editor has ever given me advice or suggestions. They just ask when they will get the next book," L'Amour chortled to Harold Keith. His millions of fans don't seem to mind. They find his books to be magic—as he, himself, found the books of others to be.

He told his daughter that he had "a time machine" in his office. The time machine, of course, was made up of the books he had assembled there—some 10,000 volumes. Later reports, in his obituaries, increased the library to 20,000. It was as if Louis L'Amour were getting in one final exaggeration. Through books, he told his daughter, she could go anywhere, at any time, and be anyone she wanted. All of this could be accomplished without ever leaving the house.

His den—the L'Amour family called it his office—was lined floor to ceiling, wall to wall, with his books of history, geography, and Western diaries. The latter he found especially nourishing. In opening the diary of some old miner or prospector, L'Amour would find immediately an authentic voice, and sometimes even a plot. He scoffed at the notion that plotting a story or novel is difficult. There are only so many plots in the history of literature, he maintained— perhaps only thirty-five in total. Once one had mastered them, one could write a book of one's choosing.

As a young girl, Angelique would enter that "office". Her father had a big black leather chair, and he would place her in it and proceed to tell her stories. Often Tina, L'Amour's faithful dog would rest at their feet. Sometimes both father and daughter would be principal characters, sharing some adventure or misadventure. She conjectures that this sense of participating in his drama was perhaps the origin of her own interest in acting.

"Listening to his exciting tales led me to see my father as quite a hero," she wrote. "Later, as I got older, I would hear stories about his own growing up, and I realized that in his own way my father was an adventurer as well as a hero."

These story sessions all took place in the L'Amour home, a Spanish style house in the fashionable Holmby Hills section of suburban Los Angeles, Bel-Air, where his neighbors included the Bing Crosby family. L'Amour's office is a cavernous 500-square foot study the size of a volley ball court. The bookcases measure 12 feet tall by 31 feet long, and are, in fact, double bookcases; they are hinged, and the fronts swing out to reveal a duplicate bookcase behind. This is the addition that his wife Kathy supervised in construction. The strong California sunlight is filtered through a high-placed rosette window. Another window overlooks the swimming pool. L'Amour's desk is placed between the fireplace and the window.

In addition to the thousands upon thousands of books neatly placed in the bookcases, there are many more piled high upon a table. This constitutes his current reading. A mountain of science magazines and history books can be found on that table at any given time. His periodical subscriptions included *Chemistry, Science, Natural History*, and *Pacific Discovery*. Because of his fame, he had access to more information than most people. NASA sent him all their releases and publications, as a matter of course. They were fuel for the outer-space frontier novel he was never to write. Of these many periodicals he confessed, "I skim them all ... I'm asked all kinds of questions by the media, and I like to have the answers." Not to show off, he added, but because people hoped he would have the answers. But L'Amour didn't consider reading work. ". . . mostly I read for the pleasure that comes with knowledge. There's so much I want to know, so many stories I have left to tell," he told *Newsweek* in 1986.

A walk around L'Amour's workroom could be unsettling. A study of the bulletin board, for instance, would reveal at least forty-five ideas for new novels, some already taking shape. He also used two IBM Selectric typewriters, one of them ten years old. There would be a different manuscript

Overlooking the ranch near Durango, Colorado.

Late night writing in the study of the ranchhouse.

Catching up on some reading in an old cock-fighting betting chair.

Inspecting the barn on the ranch.

Only a few of the many translations of L'Amour's books.

"Tina" and her master at the ranch.

Home is Bel-Air (California).

Boxing this punching bag kept L'Amour fit.

The study/library in Bel-Air where many bestsellers were written.

The Congressional Medal.

The Presidential Medal of Freedom.

The great outdoors L'Amour loved.

stuck in each. ". . . If I get sick of one, I can always work on another," he quipped. He boasted that he could work anywhere. When a visitor commented on the sound of heavy traffic which could be heard from nearby Sunset Boulevard, he remarked, "It doesn't bother me, it's like the sound of the sea." Once, as a stunt to accommodate *People* magazine, L'Amour set a table right in the middle of a traffic island on Sunset Boulevard. Then he proceeded to write. A truck driver pulled up, stopped, and the driver leaned out the window and quipped, "You've just got to be Louis L'Amour, right?"

L'Amour was very proud of the addition to his work space, and he had reason to be. Before the addition, when *The Roundup* magazine asked him for a photograph of himself at his desk, he replied that he didn't have a desk. He was making do with a borrowed table. When the addition was finished and his huge desk installed, he made a point of showing it all to visitors.

"Showing a visitor a new addition to their home, his openness and satisfaction are cut from the same cloth as the spirit he celebrates in the American West: He enjoys his success, but he doesn't need it to make him a bigger man."[4]

The rest of the house is a rambling adobe hacienda, located on a quarter-block off Sunset Boulevard. The gardens are filled with bright flowers. There are shaded patios and a covered kidney-shaped swimming pool where L'Amour worked out every day. The living room has been described as "huge," and features another fireplace.

The decor is—not surprisingly—unrelentingly Western: Indian paintings, rugs, and dolls, as well as mounted longhorns. The walls are testimony to the author's fame; many of the pieces of original art used as Bantam Book jackets festoon the walls. There is also a large oil portrait of L'Amour. Other works of art include paintings by Clifford Brycelea, a Navaho artist whom L'Amour supported and to whom he became a bit of a patron. He sponsored a Brycelea exhibition, purchased a number of his works, and was instrumental in sug-

4. Ned Smith, *American Way* magazine

gesting that one of his paintings serve as jacket art for *The Haunted Mesa*. This was a work entitled "The Sacred Navajo Prayer," which L'Amour first saw at an exhibition in the 1970s. From the moment he saw it, he said, he knew that this Native American's art was just what he needed for the cover of his novel about the Anasazi. The original painting now hangs in the L'Amour living room. Brycelea's mystical style does seem highly suitable for the ghostly and occult elements of that novel.

There were books in every room. They completely took over the cavernous bedroom, and even lined the gymnasium—an unconscious symbol of the two disparate sides of L'Amour, the bookish and the brute. In one room, two long bookshelves held his own books. "It makes me feel good to see them," he said, then modestly added, "but I'm more conscious of what I haven't done."

Other furnishings include a white football, signed by his fans on the Dallas Cowboys team, and a most unusual chair—an 18-century library chair, also known as a cockfighting chair, because it was used by the fight judge during cock matches.

L'Amour's schedule was strict and he maintained it seven days a week. He would rise at 5:30 A.M. and, after getting the two children off to school, he would spend a good six hours at the typewriter—or typewriters—before breaking for lunch. If he finished one book before his alloted writing time was up, he would put a fresh sheet of paper in the typewriter and begin another. His daily goal was five typed pages, thirty-five pages every week.

If his work went well, lunch could be a leisurely affair, either at home, or with a friend at the nearby Polo Lounge of the Beverly Hills Hotel, a chic dining room where patrons go to be seen as much as for the cuisine. It gave him satisfaction to be able to return to the location where he had really been "discovered" by the Western editor of Fawcett. As he ambled down the pink and green corridor, with its hand-painted wallpaper of huge green leaves, L'Amour was frequently recognized.

The L'Amours did a moderate amount of entertaining at home. They usually avoided the big social "Hollywood scene". L'Amour said many of their friends were people who had worked on one or more of the thirty-

plus L'Amour novels that had been scripted
into films. His closest friends and luncheon
companions included the vice president in
charge of production at Columbia Pictures,
Michael Jackson. (The *other* Michael
Jackson. This one does not wear a glove on
one hand.) Others included Ann-Margret's
attorney, a famous actress, the owner of a
primitive art gallery, a building contractor,
a TV producer, and several actor-directors.
Other friends included Dallas Cowboys
football coach Tom Landry, and Charlie
Daniels, the country-western singer. Both
used to leave the L'Amour family, house
seat tickets at the box office anytime they
played in or around Los Angeles. It made
for lively conversation around the L'Amour
fireplace. In addition, the L'Amours maintained friendships with numerous Asians
who would visit or exchange dinner invita-
tions. Some were from Japan, others from
Thailand, India and Iran. They reminded
L'Amour of his yondering days, when he
wasn't tied to a typewriter in order to
produce a minimum of three new books a
year.

Lunch at the Polo Lounge may seem
bourgeois to some. But L'Amour always

defended Hollywood, which he defined as "the name of a climate, rather than a place." L'Amour admitted to enjoying the Polo Lounge and the attentions he received there as the author of best-sellers. But as one observer concluded, "The point is, you sense that L'Amour liked to be here, but doesn't *need* to be here." One thing about Hollywood that intrigued him was that he loved the idea of being near thousands and thousands of professional writers in so small an area. Unlike some in the profession, he thought writers were the best company of all. But he did see a danger in too much fraternization. It was bad for writers to start writing for other writers, he said. "A writer should write for people, not critics or other writers."

In addition to the good feelings of being surrounded by writers, he was proud of the fact that there were, at that time, some 70,000 scientists living in the Greater Los Angeles area and in Orange County. These included employees of Lockheed, Kaiser, Hughes, Scripps, Cal Tech and others. He doubted there was a greater assemblage of talent of every kind anywhere else in the world—including New York. L'Amour also defended his choice of Beverly Hills as his permanent residence on the grounds that it was his wife's home, many of her and their friends were born there, and he liked the climate. Most important of all, "Los Angeles accepts creative people."

Whereas most writers look to New York as the center of talent and power, L'Amour was of the opposite opinion. He was quick to dismiss the New York Intellectual Establishment, which he did all his life. This attitude probably was due to the fact that his books rarely were reviewed or taken seriously by the critics until near the end of his life. He often railed against the incestuousness of living in the same buildings and going to the same parties. He would contrast one such critic, arising with a hangover in the morning, and looking at himself pale-faced in the mirror, and wondering what he was going to do next, with people who *knew* what they were going to do next. They were the doers of this world, and he wrote for the people who made things happen, not the effete who merely stood around and commented upon it. He would agree with novelist Norman Mailer, who defined critics as "eunuchs at a gang-bang." Perhaps thinking of novelist John Updike, whose *Couples* had made a big splash, L'Amour said critics praised books as literature when all they were about was what a couple did in bed, while his books were dismissed when they traced the opening up of an entire continent.

Whether lunch was at home or at the Polo Lounge, afternoons would find L'Amour working out with weights and a punching bag. He would struggle lifting 300 pounds, and punch until he was arm-weary. He kept his weight around 220 pounds. After a swim and a shower, he would return to his "office" in the afternoon and do research on one of the numerous projects he had going simultaneously. "I'm doing research on a few books now that I possibly won't write for ten years," he told a 1980 interviewer. By his own reckoning, he read over 300 books a year and scanned about 400 more. The only time he ever read fiction, he said, was when he traveled by plane. He also regularly read thirty different magazines. He would read well into the night, until he fell asleep with the book or magazine in his lap, like the little boy in Jamestown, whose mother would then remove the book and turn off the light.

He never stopped working. "People ask me how I can do so much, and I wonder why I have done so little." This is either extreme modesty or disingenuousness.

Despite his rigorous writing schedule, life was not all work. He pursued his interests in archaeology and wildlife, and he was a devoted family man. His favorite kind of relaxation was a trip through the Western wilderness with his gear in a backpack, hiking his beloved mountains. His family accompanied him on many of these trips. He was keen to find unexplored land, and his son Beau took dramatic photographs of unpopulated vistas viewed from a plane he and his father flew over Colorado, Wyoming, and Utah.

"You cannot write about the West without living in it," he believed. So the L'Amour family spent a lot of time in the countryside near Caliente Creek as well as a month in Colorado every year—thinking and following old mountain trails. He liked to quote one of his favorite poets, the Californian Robinson Jeffers: "When the cities lie at the monster's feet, there are left the mountains." When crossing the desert, L'Amour preferred vehicles with 4-wheel drive.

Between 1956 and 1960, he published eleven novels, an incredible feat of will as well as of creativity. These are *The Burning Hills* (1956), *Silver Canyon* (1956), *Sitka* (1957), *Last Stand at Papago Wells* (1957), *The Tall Stranger* (1957), *Radigan* (1958), *The First Fast Draw* (1959), *Taggart* (1959), *Flint* (1960), and *Day Breakers* (1960).

Also during this period, six films were made from his novels. These included *The Tall Stranger* (1957), starring Joel McCrea and Virginia Mayo; *Utah Blaine* (1958), starring Rory Calhoun; *Guns of the Timberlands* (1960), starring Alan Ladd and Jeanne Crain and produced and co-scripted by Aaron Spelling; and most notably, the only Western ever directed by the legendary George Cukor, *Heller in Pink Tights* (1960), featuring Anthony Quinn and Sophia Loren. This, of course, was the film version of L'Amour's off-beat 1955 novel, *Heller With a Gun*. Recalling the adventures of a theater company touring the West in the 1880s, it was a genteel spoof of Westerns which just missed the mark. L'Amour, however, adored the film. It was his second-favorite film made from his work, after *Hondo*. Of Heller he said in conversation, "Couldn't have been improved," which is surely the highest accolade.

But for L'Amour, the most important event to take place during this period was the publication of *Day Breakers*, the very first of the Sackett novels. L'Amour had made his giant leap from writing individual novels to beginning an enormous inter-related saga. As ambitious as Balzac's *The Human Comedy*, L'Amour's family saga— or sagas, as there came to be three separate ones—were to have included fifty frontier novels about three families: The Sacketts, the Chantrys, and the Talons. Only death kept him from realizing this huge ambition. Most people could not conceive of typing that many pages, let alone writing them!

L'Amour related the circumstances which led to the inspiration for the Sackett saga. In "A Special Interview with Louis L'Amour," which appeared as an appendix to *Comstock Lode*, he tells how he was down in Tucumcari, New Mexico, and became engaged in a fight in the town square. He was winning until two of his opponent's cousins—from two different families—joined in. After the fracas was settled, he became friends with the two male cousins. They rode across the country that night, and after setting up camp, talked about the fight. One of them confessed, "We never have any fights." The reason being— in one version—that the one cousin had thirteen boys in his family and the other had sixteen. The notion of a huge family that always came to the rescue of one another appealed to L'Amour. "I began thinking about it and I decided to write a story about a family like that, where whenever one of them was in trouble, all the others came to help." And that is precisely what he did in creating the Sacketts. In *Ride the River* he wrote, "If you step on one Sackett's toes, they all came running."

While L'Amour claimed he didn't really have any favorite among his novels—the one on which he currently was working, invariably was his "favorite"—he did admit to having a special place in his heart for the Sackett novels. "My wife, Kathy, still enjoys reminding me of how exhilarated I was when I was writing that first Sackett novel, how I would come bounding up the stairs to read her practically every page fresh from my typewriter."[5]

After a number of novels with Sackett brothers and cousins as characters in the West following the Civil War, L'Amour's fan mail was filled with letters from readers who had become smitten with his Sackett family history and lore. They actually wanted to know more about the earlier pioneers, the Sacketts' forebears. L'Amour says then that "I knew I had to go back in time to tell the story of the first Sacketts and how they came to settle in America."

This of course explains the lack of chronological order to the Sackett volumes, not to mention the fact that L'Amour was always involved with many projects, and not just *The Sacketts*. Of these novels about the progenitors, *Sacketts' Land* is concerned with the patriarch, Barnabas Sackett, who left England in 1599 for the New World. The story of Barnabas and his wife, Abigail, continues in *To the Far Blue*

5. "A Message from Louis L'Amour," *The Walking Drum*

Mountains. In that work the reader meets their three oldest sons, Kin-Ring, Yance, and Jubal as well. Kin-Ring's and Yance's stories are depicted in *The Warrior's Path*, but Jubal was given an entire volume of his own, whose title is his name. The longest Sackett novel, *Jubal Sackett*, became another mammoth best-seller.

Jubal Sackett has one of L'Amour's typical openings, in which the reader is immediately plunged into the action with no fanfare:

"A cold wind blew off Hanging Dog Mountain and I had no fire, nor dared I strike so much as a spark that might betray my hiding place. Somewhere near an enemy lurked, waiting." Immediately, the reader wants to know: Who is this person? What is he doing there? And who is his enemy?

L'Amour used Jubal as emblematic of the kind of man who opened up the frontier. He goes over the mountain to leave home as he knows it, in what would later be Tennessee. He has to find out what is out there, in unchartered territory. L'Amour uses Jubal's adventures to get his readers to see and experience just what it was like to be one of the first white people to see this country when it was virgin and unexplored. The novel also gives L'Amour ample opportunity to display his knowledge of Indian history. We meet the complex society of the Natchee tribe, who call themselves children of the sun, and the horrifying Commanches. Jubal falls in love with the daughter of the Great Sun, who becomes missing. His search for her gives him his most challenging experiences.

In writing about the composition of *Jubal Sackett*, L'Amour took pride in stating, "I think you will find it has lots of facts and feelings about the early days of this country, lots of detail . . ."

Lots of detail indeed! In his later novels, L'Amour took his role to be not only a storyteller and an entertainer, but also an edifier.

In *The Country Gentleman* magazine he is quoted as saying, "The average guy is kind of confined in his job and is limited as to how much he can learn. Even the average university professor has become too specialized in this age of specialization. So I see myself as a kind of funnel through which a lot of knowledge is flowing to other people."

And funnel it did. His plots—and some-times all suspense—would be interrupted by set pieces on the making of Madeira wine, the building of fires, the production of nails, the moisture in cacti, patronage in Elizabethan England, Buffalo behavior, bird calls, Swiss militia, vagarities of the weather, and, above all, frontier facts, of which he had an inexhaustible supply.

Once, he placed a certain make of gun in one of his novels—knowing it was an eso-teric item made only in limited supply. So he placed a footnote on the page, justifying his use of such a gun. An editor decided a footnote in a novel was uncalled for, and deleted it. When the novel was published, L'Amour received a deluge of mail from readers, thinking they had, finally, tripped him up on a factual detail. There was no such gun, they insisted. L'Amour had to write each and explain his illuminating footnote had been removed without his knowledge. After that, his editors didn't tinker with his historical facts—and there were thousands. Referring to L'Amour's image of himself as a "kind of funnel," John D. Nesbitt quipped, "in his later novels, such as *Sackett's Land, Rivers West, Fair*

Blows the Wind, The Proving Trail, and *Bendigo Shafter*, the funnel becomes something of a wide-mouthed chute . . ."

Allied to his encyclopedic passages on Western (and British and Far Eastern) history, L'Amour is expert at identifying early explorers of any region, and giving histories of forts, towns and cities—including Manhattan. Sometimes these are handled in casual asides, but often he has his fearful erudition coming trippingly off the tongue of local old timers. As Robert L. Gale rather sardonically wrote of one such passage in *Lonely on the Mountain*, "I'd say the old coot had been foraging in L'Amour's L.A. library." As L'Amour himself did, every day.

When L'Amour was perhaps in the middle of telling the Sackett saga—around 1974—he publicly announced an even bigger scheme:

"Some time ago, I decided to tell the story of the American frontier through the eyes of three families—fictional families, but with true and factual experiences. The names I chose were Sackett, Chantry, and Talon . . . Story by story, generation by generation, these families are moving westward. When the journeys are ended and the forty-odd are completed, the reader should have a fairly true sense of what happened on the American frontier.''[6]

And L'Amour's ambition did not stop there. In 1984, at the age of 76, he published *The Walking Drum*, which was said to be the first volume of a trilogy devoted to the Kerbouchards. No American writer, not even James T. Farrell, with his immense *Silence of History* series, was as ambitious.

Family has always been a subject important to L'Amour. He believed strongly in the old adage that blood is thicker than water. In a competitive world, the family comes first. William Tell Sackett, hero of numerous L'Amour novels, is always just as concerned about his mother's comfort as he is about his own chances of surviving the next gunfight. L'Amour also believed that what a man becomes is partially due to who his ancestors have been. In addition, he felt that the only way children learn how to be adult men and women is by observing their parents. The family unit is the support system, an educational and a moral system in his novels.

6. Preface to *Sackett's Land*, pp. v-vi

The image of the home and the hearth are important in all his fiction, not just the family sagas. In *Hondo*, the hero remembers "a long meadow fresh with new-cut hay, a house where smoke would soon again rise from the chimney, and where shadows would gather . . . and beside him a woman held in her arms a sleeping child . . . a woman who would be there with him, in that house, before that hearth." In this one passage he posits both images.

Elsewhere, in *Westward the Tide*, he extols the virtues of the sound of rain on a roof, the look of fire in the fireplace, and the feel of a woman in his arms. Warmth and closeness are the two things in this world that matter most. L'Amour's adherence to the solid, old-fashioned virtues of family ties may in part account for his huge popularity with the common reader.

His Sackett family is frequently uprooted and transported from Eastern soil to the West, but they emerge with all their civilized traits intact. The Sackett's idealistic and romantic attitudes help them survive on the frontier.

The Sackett family tree is divided into three major branches: The Smoky Mountain Sacketts, the Cumberland Gap Sacketts, and the Clinch Mountain Sacketts. All come from the Tennessee mountains, but there are primary differences among them. The Smoky Mountain Sacketts are gentlemen, most notably William Tell Sackett, who one critic—Michael T. Marsden—has dubbed "the Abraham Lincoln of the Western landscape." The Cumberland Gap Sacketts are to be trusted, but are less memorable. And the Clinch Mountain Sacketts, as personified by the gun-fighting brothers, Logan and Nolan, can be ornery. Yet, true to the vision L'Amour had the day he saw a family of men rush to a brother's aid, they can, to a man, be trusted to help any Sackett who is in trouble, regardless of which side of the law he happens to be on at the time.

In an essay in *North Dakota Quarterly*, Marsden concludes,

"These formal family groups may well constitute the most ambitious and complex attempt to date to create a Faulknerian series of interrelated characters and events in the popular Western tradition." He goes on to say, "L'Amour seems to be able to create in his readers a feeling of belonging to a tradition; this in turn provides

L'Amour with the basis for a popular, organic fiction that creates the formulaic Western world."

This is all true. It is to be regretted, however, that L'Amour did not conceive his family sagas well in advance of writing the individual volumes. The books have not been issued in anything resembling an orderly fashion. As it stands, there exist gaps in the story line which are frustrating and confusing.

After the first Sackett novel, *Day Breakers*, L'Amour published *Flint*, which also appeared in 1960. It was followed by *Sackett* (1961), *Shalako* (1962), *Killoe* (1962), *High Lonesome* (1962), *Lando* (1962), *Fallon* (1963), and *How the West Was Won* (1963). At this time, L'Amour's novels averaged 150 pages, with the exception of the ambitious, five-part *How the West Was Won*. Most L'Amour aficionados believe that the blockbuster 1962 film was made from a L'Amour novel. Actually, the reverse is true. L'Amour produced, in 1963, a novelization of James R. Webb's film script. The film had been released a year earlier, in 1962.

The film featured an all-star cast, ranging from Debbie Reynolds and Carroll Baker, to Lee J. Cobb and Henry Fonda, to Karl

Malden and Gregory Peck, to James Stewart and John Wayne. That's just for starters. Even Andy Devine and Thelma Ritter had roles! The narrator was Spencer Tracy. It was a cast as big as the West itself. Webb won an Academy Award for his script, and his vision and structure doubtless helped produce one of L'Amour's longest and most cohesive books.

In 1967, L'Amour was asked to lecture at the University of Oklahoma, as part of their annual professional writing conference. Although he was never officially a student there, he did regard the engagement as a kind of homecoming. On June 7, he addressed a nearly-packed auditorium in Norman: "Hit your reader on the chin," he exclaimed. "So he knows he's in a story. The reader doesn't want to know what's *going* to happen. He wants to know what's happening *now*."

He went on to say that most of life is dull, so readers want something that will lift them out of themselves. He spoke in short, abrupt phrases that came out like gunshots: "Make something happen. Ideas are all around. Think. Develop. Get the reader interested. Then the plot will carry you along." His talk was the very opposite of a professorial lecture. It was totally devoid of critical jargon.

The speech was also full of examples: "Every sentence must have a feeling as well as a fact, like 'Chip rode with caution.' " As L'Amour stood there, he himself looked like a character out of one of his own novels. Over six feet tall, weighing over 200 pounds, barrel-chested and with a square, weathered face, his eyes were deep set and hazel, his curly hair dark. As he gestured, one could not help but notice that his hands were massive and strong, like those of a cattleman or a miner. L'Amour had been both. In his gait he was big, expansive, and lumbering. He punched the air for emphasis.

It was clear he identified with his fictional heroes, who were also big. Speaking to the *Washington Post*, he said, "I write about the big man because I know myself and my own body . . . Anyway, people like big heroes." However big he was physically, he could never be big enough critically. Of the lack of reviews of his books he told the *Post*, "You find that all the way around . . . You know, Poe and Whittier had their problems, too. Poe was recognized by the French before the Eastern types thought he was okay. The literary establishment is very ingrown. Numbers of them live in the same building. It's insular and it's parochial."

L'Amour remained confident that when future historians and critics look back on what elements made the West, his books will be considered seminal sources. "I hope that someday people will look at me and realize what an amazing thing I did." Modesty was not always his forte. "I don't know if any writer has ever taken on the scope I've taken on. I am trying to bring the West's history out of the myths from the very beginning."

Once, on a television program, L'Amour was asked what was the one particular quality that the Western man had. He seemed stumped for an answer. Later, off camera, with hindsight, the answer came to him: "Dignity. The Western people had it. They were poor, but they had pride and dignity. A man might steal your horse, but he wouldn't lie to you. He would tell you to your face he stole it."

During the late 1960s, at the height of the Vietnam War, Louis L'Amour realized his books were giving American GIs a sense of dignity and pride even as they were caught up in that conflict. This realization came when he received over four hundred letters from servicemen, who said in various ways that they found relief from daily cynicism in his books and stories. One young man, a writer named Steve Mason, sent L'Amour a volume of his own poetry. He inscribed it as follows:

"For Louis L'Amour,

Because on nights I thought would be my last, I did not write letters home or say my prayers. I simply read a Louis L'Amour, and daybreak always found me ready and hopeful. Such is your wisdom and your courage. Yours is the most human of hearts. Thanks for being who you are . . ."

L'Amour was inordinately proud of his fan mail—which numbered in the thousands of letters every year—and other vestiges of the effect he had upon readers. He discovered that in the book trading sessions that went on within the Tehachapi prison in California, where it took five of any other to get one by L'Amour.

A visitor to his home would be shown proof of the range of his readership. In a photograph of a sixth grade Canadian school class each pupil was shown holding a copy of a different L'Amour book, which was required reading in its history program. Another document was a letter from the chairman of the Earth Sciences Department at Stanford University, who was seeking information from L'Amour. The author estimated, that at any given time, there were five or six individuals writing Ph.D dissertations on his *oeuvre*.

In 1968, the film version of *Shalako* was released. It starred Sean Connery, Brigitte Bardot, Stephen Boyd, Jack Hawkins and Honor Blackman (of James Bond's "Pussy Galore" fame). The film was given a Royal Premiere in London, and L'Amour got himself together and attended. That evening he was presented to Princess Margaret. He appeared on the "Merv Griffin Show" in 1971, and, in 1972, published the first Chantry novel, *North to the Rails*. The first Tallon novel, *Rivers West*, would not appear until 1975. By then, there were over

32,000,000 copies of his books in print. That year L'Amour surpassed Bantam Book's previous best-selling writer, John Steinbeck. Steinbeck, a Nobel Prize winner, had sold a mere 41,300,000 copies. L'Amour appeared on the "Today Show" to boast about his success.

The next year he appeared on "60 Minutes" and waxed eloquent about things Western. Interviewed by Morley Safer, he debunked numerous myths about the West, and reiterated his belief that the movies over-dramatized the role of the gunfighter in the frontier. All in all, it was a disappointing show for anyone familiar with L'Amour's history. He tended to repeat the same stories he trotted forth in each interview, including the grandfather who fought off Indians while settling his homestead in North Dakota. He looked physically fit, however, and was filmed working out with his punching bag in his home gym. By now, his long sideburns were grey, but his fierce eyebrows remained black. His face was jowly; he was 68 years old. The program showed brief cuts of L'Amour walking with his wife, son and daughter along a trail in Colorado. But his family barely registers with the viewer. The show was all Louis. It has been rebroadcast at least twice since, the most recent date being September 11, 1988.

Honors began to flow in. One of the most meaningful was an Honorary Doctorate in Literature, given to L'Amour in 1972 by Jamestown College, back in his home state of North Dakota. Not bad for a high-school drop-out! That same year, he was named a Theodore Roosevelt Rough Rider by the State of North Dakota.

In a 1977 survey of the Twenty-five Best Westerns of All Time, conducted by The Western Writers of America, two of L'Amour's titles were among the twenty-five: *Hondo* and *Flint*.

And in 1978, another meaningful award was bestowed: He was awarded the Great Seal of the Ute Tribe. This was highly appropriate, given L'Amour's compassionate view of Native Americans. He believed the white man's mistake was to try to convert them to his own beliefs:

"First we should study what they believe and how it applies to the way they live," he wrote in *The Lonesome Gods*, one of his most autobiographical books. He held that the Indians' own religion had served them well, and there was no need to inflict the white man's religion upon them. He recognized that Indians respected a fighter and despised a coward. They had great patience and could outwait the white man, whose restlessness so often was his own undoing. L'Amour wrote that the Indians had great pride in their handicraft, and great courage, and great wit. Above all, unlike the white man, they were not materialistic, seeking only stronger medicines, greater wisdom, and internal powers.

"In the Old West," he told the *New York Times*, "many white men who knew nothing about Indians hated them and many white men who were better acquainted with Indians liked them better. Unhappily, too many of the white men saw the Indian after his culture had begun to break down."

Many writers of Westerns treat the Indians as a malevolent force of nature. Not L'Amour. He recognized their cultural complexity and even their sense of humor. In *Sackett's Land*, Barnabas Sackett, the clan's grand sire, posited the family attitude—and by inference, the L'Amour attitude—toward the Native Americans:

"Dealing with Indians I found them of shrewd intelligence, quick to detect the false, quick to appreciate quality, quick to resent contempt and to appreciate bravery. So much of the Indian's life was predicated upon courage that he respected it above all else. He needed courage in the hunt, and in warfare, and to achieve success with the tribe he needed both courage and wit."

Showing what led to the white man's various difficulties with the Indians was high on L'Amour's list of priorities in his frontier fiction. He felt he actually could correct some of the major misunderstandings and miscalculations. "You see," he said in his conversation with Marsden, "actually this is never dwelled upon, but many treaties were broken by the Indians also."

What L'Amour advocated was that we look at the Indian in human and sociological terms: "To be a man in an Indian tribe you had to be a warrior. To be a warrior you had to have killed an enemy in battle or to have at least struck a living enemy and gotten away with it. Then you could speak in the Council, then you were a man whose opinions were respected. The old men were the establishment, and when the white man comes along they are ready to make peace. They see it as necessary. But the changes happen so rapidly that there is no other way in the culture for the young Indian to become a man. So while the old Indian makes peace, the young Indian makes war."

It was, in its way, a double bind. L'Amour held that if the white man had not moved West so quickly, and in such great numbers, the Indian in all probability could have made cultural adjustments. They might even have found some other way for a young Indian to gain warrior status.

But the white man came in too many numbers. Powder-Face, an Indian in *Treasure Mountain* (1972), reminisces on the phenomenon:

"We killed them and killed them and killed them, and still they came. It was not the horse soldiers that whipped us, it was not the death of the buffalo, nor the white man's cows. It was the people. It was the families.

"The rest we might conquer, but the people kept coming and they built their lodges where no Indian could live."

Because of the sheer numbers of the white man, and his willfulness, the Indian was doomed to surrender. Eventually, L'Amour would be honored for his compassionate vision of the Native American.

In the meantime, other honors followed. His 1979 novel, *Bendigo Shafter*, received an American Book Award in the Western category, a category that no longer exists today. This was pleasing to L'Amour, even though *Publisher's Weekly* had reviewed that novel the previous January, and found its plotting loose and its story more rambling than in the best of L'Amour. Also in 1979, he received a Golden Plate Award for *The Iron Marshall*. That book carries one of the most curious (and longest) dedications of any book in recent times. Over two full pages, L'Amour lists his dedicatees—the names of the entire sales department of Bantam Books. He knew, as the saying goes, which side his bread was buttered on.

In 1981, *Saturday Review* named L'Amour one of the world's Five Best-Selling Authors. The others were Harold Robbins, Barbara Cartland, Irving Wallace—who had done a screenplay based on one of L'Amour's novels, *The Burning Hills*—

and Janet Dailey. At the time, L'Amour had 110,000,000 copies in print, and had had 78 novels published. Also, in the same year, L'Amour received the Golden Saddleman Award, for outstanding contributions to the history and legend of the West. Members of the Western Writers' Association vote for the recipient. The award was presented by Bud Johns, vice president for corporate communications of Levi-Straus, at the climax of the 1981 awards banquet in Santa Rosa, California. From the din of applause, L'Amour obviously was a very popular choice. Previously he had won a Golden Spur Award from the same group in 1968 for his novel, *Down the Long Hills*, one of his more freshly plotted novels. It is also one of L'Amour's best-organized novels in terms of unities of time and place. The action is also less diffuse, due to there being only eight main characters. Its heroes are seven-year-old Hardy Collins; his young three-year-old companion, Betty Sue Powell; Hardy's father, Scott; two mountain men; two white thugs; and some Indians. The plot revolves around how the young boy and girl must survive in the wilderness and locate Hardy's father after everyone else in their wagon train has been massacred. The brief novel is, among other things, about survival and resourcefulness, and the bond between father and son. If one were to select an early L'Amour novel to honor, it would be a fine choice.

Such was Louis L'Amour's popularity, that the day *The Lonesome Gods*—his longest book at 450 pages—was published in 1983, it already was in its fourth hardcover printing, with a total of 155,000 copies distributed in advance. At that time, his top sellers were, in this order:

Hondo, 2.3 million copies in print; *Sackett*, 2.121 million; *Flint*, 1.95 million; *The First Fast Draw*, 1.87 million; *The Burning Hills*, 1.83 million; *Day Breakers*, 1.83 million (a tie); *The Sackett Brland*, 1.82 million; *Mohave Crossing*, 1.75 million; and *Lando*, 1.65 million. Surprisingly, *How the West Was Won* is not among the top ten.

Of these phenomenal sales, Oscar Dystel, Bantam's president, said: "There's a degree of absolute certainty in the sale of a L'Amour book . . . We often operate on the assumption that 45% of the books we send to bookstores will eventually be returned. With Lous L'Amour, the returns are usually about 12%, among the lowest in the publishing industry."

"Our customers actually harass us for new titles," said Harold Gloff of the B. Dalton Booksellers chain. And the demand is not restricted by any means to American fans. The books are translated into French, Polynesian, Swedish, Danish, Norwegian, Portuguese, Japanese, Italian, Greek, Dutch, and Serbo-Croatian, among other languages. In 1976 he proudly added a Chinese translation to the list.

All these sales were not unaided by the publisher or by L'Amour himself. In addition to his numerous television appearances, L'Amour engaged in personal appearances. He became, in Morley Safer's words, "The noble savage of the literary luncheon." In 1975, he moseyed into the canyons of New York City for several days, to increase his visibility in the East. That was the year he appeared on the "Today Show," gave interviews, held a new conference, and attended the American Booksellers Association's 75th Anniversary Convention, held in May at the New York Hilton and Americana hotels. The event was attended by 12,000 booksellers, publishers, and assorted book collectors—plus dozens of authors hyping their wares. These included Leo Durocher, Edwin Newman, and Erica Wilson. L'Amour autographed books for hours, prompting one wag to declare that the most valuable book in New York that week was an un-autographed Louis L'Amour.

In one interview at that time, L'Amour confessed that he never read Western novels himself. He was afraid he might inadvertently copy somebody else's plot or characters. He also said that whenever he was away from writing for more than three days, he began to itch.

By far the most spectacular of L'Amour's personal appearances occurred in 1980, to celebrate the printing of the 100-millionth copy of his books. He took to the road in a 1972 Luxury Custom Silver Eagle bus, bearing a Western mural on both sides. Inside, the vehicle featured a master bedroom, living room, sofa, TV, VCR, stereo, bathroom and kitchen. He was travelling in the style made famous by country and western music performers. The bus was called "The Louis L'Amour Overland Express," and it made news, even in the *New York Times*.

For three event-packed weeks in June, L'Amour endured a grueling tour. The first leg of the journey was to eight midwestern cities—Chicago, Moline, East Moline, and Rock Island in Illinois, Des Moines and Davenport in Iowa, Omaha, Nebraska, and Kansas City, Missouri. The second leg of the journey took him to Nashville and Knoxville in Tennessee, Little Rock, Arkansas, Tulsa and Oklahoma City in Oklahoma. In Knoxville, he was made an honorary citizen of the state. In Nashville, he was saluted both in words and music by the Charlie Daniels Band at the Grand Ole Opry. In the heartland of America, L'Amour was king. Everywhere he reigned from his gleaming tour bus, surrounded by crates of his books. He greeted booksellers, charmed TV talk show hosts, and posed for photographs, always wearing Western garb, including sometimes a turquoise medallion the size of a horseshoe. If he appeared potbellied, no one minded a bit. If his Western costumes annoyed those who disliked conspicuousness, they delighted his fans and pleased his family and friends, who took his dress to be an element of self-mocking excess, or proof of his dedication to authenticity. He accepted keys to the cities of Davenport, Des Moines, Omaha, and Kansas City. Above all, he autographed copies of his 75 books then in print, especially copies of his two newest titles, *Yondering* and *The Warrior's Path*. The latter was the fifteenth volume of his Sackett saga.

What L'Amour did probably better than any other living writer was to work the distribution personnel. "Louis is a book salesman's dream," Louis Satz, sales director for Bantam Books, said. "He's met and worked with all 140 of our fulltime sales people and he cultivates the wholesalers who are the people who decide which books get rack space." And Arthur Jacobs, the general manager of a bookstore in San Diego, agreed. Because his salesmen were charmed by L'Amour, they made certain his titles were in stock in the stores. With 100 to 500 different titles coming out every month, it made a difference.

The "Louis L'Amour Overland Express" and its authentic cowboy especially visited truck stops of America, where devoted readers waited in long lines for him to sign their copies of his books. Some of the men waiting asked that he sign the books "for my son" rather than for themselves, a familiar ploy by those too shy to admit they were addicted to Westerns themselves. On the other hand, the predominance of ten-gallon hats and cowboy boots at the truck stops would seem to indicate that all truck drivers are, at heart, cowboys.

One truck driver from Marston, Missouri, wearing a straw cowboy hat, told a reporter: "I'll tell you why I like his books ... If he says Gus the bartender tended bar in someplace in 1876, you can believe that there was such a town and that there was a bar there and that a man named Gus was for truth the bartender."

Almost everyone found L'Amour modest and direct. He looked right at you when he spoke, with no evasiveness. His square, jutting jaw gave him a look of solidity. One editor recalled, "I've seen him at banquets where everyone is preening his tail feathers, but not him. He doesn't need to."

For all of that, others found him to be quite sophisticated. This is Gene Alfonsi's impression. "Urbane" is the word Alfonsi used to describe him. He found L'Amour to be more Beverly Hills than Beverly Hills hillbilly. Alfonsi is President and CEO of

Scherer Investments Group, a major book and magazine distributor. He was also President of E.P.A.—the Educational Paperback Association. In that capacity, he discussed L'Amour's work with the man. He found him to be very eager to get his books into the schools—not as Westerns, but as histories. He believed they should be part of the curriculum. Alfonsi reaffirms L'Amour's position that he wished to be taken seriously as a historian. After meeting L'Amour, he began to read Westerns—a genre he never before had approached.

In 1981, L'Amour received three awards —the Buffalo Bill Award, the National Genealogical Society Award, and the Distinguished Newsboy Award. The same year saw him break out of the mass market corral when Bantam published his novel, *Comstock Lode*, simultaneously in both trade paperback and hard cover editions. It was his first trade paperback ever. When asked, he could not remember whether *Comstock Lode* was his 78th or 79th book, explaining—once again—that he produced three books every year.

"People sometimes marvel at the way I produce," he told Edwin McDowell of the *New York Times*. "But I don't. You'll find many composers who have produced far more proportionately [*sic.*] than I have. And Shakespeare wrote thirty-six plays and a lot of poetry at the same time he was acting in two plays a week. Later he even helped to manage a theater, all the while producing two masterpieces a year."

The comparison to Shakespeare, while meant only in terms of productivity, is the kind of remark L'Amour would make which caused certain critics to take umbrage. Late in life L'Amour had taken to writing prefaces and introductions to his novels, and in a number he had referred to Homer in comparison to his own story-telling compulsion and creation of sagas. This led one critic, John D. Nesbitt, to label L'Amour a "paper mâché Homer", and to suggest that L'Amour was the Zane Grey of his age, not the Homer.

Homer was not the only literary figure that L'Amour invoked in his own defense. In the pages of *Newsweek* in 1986, he was touchy about having written 95 books by that time. "That big number can give the wrong impression. Critics forget that Dickens and Balzac were prolific and that Noël Coward wrote one of his best plays [*Hay Fever*] in 24 hours . . . There are some, you know, who don't think I write fast *enough*."

Comparing Noël Coward with Louis L'Amour has to be one of the strangest pronouncements in recent literary history. The fact that he wrote defensive prefaces to his later books suggests that L'Amour was still upset with the critics for not giving him what he felt was his due. In his introduction to *Yondering*, for instance, he states blatantly, "I had no desire to write to please those who made it their business to comment but for the people who do the work of the world." In *Bendigo Shafter*, he has a character make the fine distinction between "scholarship" and "knowledge"— which he says is "often a different thing." In the same *Yondering* introduction he makes this shot from the hip: "Many of those who comment on writing done by others sometimes know surprisingly little about writing itself and how it is done."

L'Amour had a long-standing dislike, or distrust, of critics, particularly critics who lived in New York City. It was not such a problem in his early days. His novels were published as paperback originals, and according to the tradition of the time, were rarely reviewed, as hardcover books were. Nor were they ordered by many libraries; mass-market paperbacks were thought too ephemeral both in content and binding to be of value in library collections. As L'Amour's fans grew to the millions, however, librarians found they had to stock his paperback originals as well as the later hardcover novels.

It is ironic that the early work was scantily reviewed, because most critics taking an overview of his accomplishments are of the opinion that his early Western fiction constitutes his best work. Most of them were only around 150 pages in length and were lean as their heroes, while admittedly marred by being written to formula. *Hondo* is the novel most often admired as his best. Critics also feel that *How the West Was Won* was a tauter, more ordered novel than most L'Amours. *Flint* has its champions as well.

But even when critics praise him, it is most often qualified praise. As J.D. Reed wrote, "It would do a disservice to make extravagant claims for this Western man; he is hardly a Whitman, voicing our collective unconscious." Then Reed does go on to opine, "New readers of the Sackett novels can discover the beliefs of the silent, moral, or just plain nostalgic majority—and have a rip-roaring time in the process."

Other critics are less kind. Don D. Walker, in his "The Scholar as Mountain Man," dismisses L'Amour's thinking as "shallow and fatuous." Ernest Bulow, in "Still Tall in the Saddle: Louis L'Amour's Classic Western Hero," takes potshots at L'Amour's need "to conform to popular taste and to keep up with shifts in public sentiment," a charge of sycophancy which L'Amour felt compelled to refute in a foreword to *The Strong Shall Live*. It's as if he felt compelled to answer his critics at every turn.

Further critical voices were raised. John D. Nesbitt, in the pages of *Western American Literature*, charged that in the later Sackett novels, the entertainment value of L'Amour's books had been diminished by an "overbearing design." In the same magazine, William Bloodworth charged L'Amour's flamboyant *Fair Blows the Wind* was an egregious and "obvious attempt to top the historical fiction market." This was not the first charge of exploitation of the audience. Earlier, Hank Nuwer, in his 1976 review of *Rivers West*, saw that book as an attempt at capitalizing upon the nation's "bicentennial sentiment." And Robert L. Gale, who devoted years to researching the first book-length critical study of the author, nevertheless felt compelled to castigate L'Amour for not branching out, not being innovative, not taking risks. As Gale points out, even his great departure, in *The Walking Drum* was not marketed as a great departure, for fear—according to Gale—that "sales figures might slump."

This last criticism may be unfair. After all, a writer—even one as popular as L'Amour—seldom has any say in how his books are marketed. That is the job of the publisher. And in writing *The Walking Drum*, he did indeed make a departure from the American frontier, as he did later in *Last of the Breed*.

Like *Fair Blows the Wind*, *The Walking Drum* (1984) is a swashbuckler but this time set in 12th-century Europe and Asia. It begins in Brittany and proceeds to Spain, returns to France, thrusts onward to Flanders, Kiev, the Black Sea, Constantinople and Tabriz. It has, as used to be said of epic films, a cast of thousands. L'Amour proclaimed it to be the first volume of a promised Middle Eastern medieval trilogy. To write it, he read—by his count—several thousand books on the Middle Ages, covering everything from costumes to cuisine. He had twenty books in his office on costume alone. He already knew the territory first-hand, he said, from his travels—but not its history. He also made a number of trips to Europe and the Far East to research the book first-hand.

A departure indeed, but publication of *The Walking Drum* in 1984 was a bit misleading. He had written it fifteen years before, but his publisher had persuaded him to put it on the shelf. It wasn't a Western, after all, and Louis L'Amour was known for his Westerns. Speaking of that publisher, L'Amour crowed to *USA Today*: "He didn't know what a favor he was doing me. Because now it's worth a good deal more money than it was then." *The Walking Drum* was the #1 hardcover bestseller and spent 16 weeks on the *New York Times* list.

Last of the Breed (1986) also was a #1 best-seller, and at the time was L'Amour's biggest hardcover seller ever, only to be surplanted by *The Haunted Mesa* when it was published in 1987. It then became L'Amour's biggest hardcover seller ever.

Last of the Breed featured a United States Air Force Major nicknamed Joe Mack, whose experimental aircraft is forced down over the Bering Sea by Russians. Joe Mack happens to be part Sioux, and he uses his wits and heritage to escape a top-security prison and survive in Siberia, as only "a true Indian born out of his time" could. There is much slaughter of animals, tanning of hides, and crafting of moccasins. Alan Gelb, who reviewed the novel in the *New York Times Book Review*, concluded, that, "Like Sylvester Stallone, another American folk hero, Mr. L'Amour has found himself revered and remunerated in a hospitable climate which values ready-made myths about Americans, single-handedly dispatching our creepy foreign enemies."

By injecting a native American into a foreign espionage plot, however, L'Amour did reveal that he had more than one arrow in his quiver. In a national news magazine,

L'Amour stated he had conceived the modern story of conflict between the superpowers partly in response to those who dismiss him as a latter-day Zane Grey. "I don't like being pigeonholed," he complained. "I don't like people saying they've got any*one* or any*thing* figured out completely." Despite its front-page references to Gorbachev and Soviet Jewry, the book is L'Amour's old formula placed in a different setting. The hero is, once again, well-read and passionately driven to "keep looking over the horizon."

In the summer of 1987, L'Amour published yet another "breakthrough" novel, *The Haunted Mesa*. This was a departure because it was a combination of a Western and an occult tale. It centered about a legend that long had fascinated L'Amour—the mystery of the Anasazi, the race of cliff-dwellers who simply vanished off the face of the earth. Their remains have been found in all four states of the Four Corners—Utah, Colorado, Arizona and New Mexico.

L'Amour wrote lovingly of these people in his chapter titled "The Old Ones" in *Frontier*, three years earlier in 1984. Now he was paying tribute, in a way, to the cave dwellers in his fiction. The book drew on his wide knowledge of Indian lore and mysticism, as well as his love for and knowledge of the Four Corners' country. It was another detailed epic, exploring the question of what was the evil from which the Anasazi fled, and what could be so terrible, that an entire people would leave everything behind? But the book was marred by repetition.

Critical commentary on these late novels was not all negative. Not by a long shot. Of *The Walking Drum*, the Chicago *Sun-Times* wrote that it was "enormously powerful storytelling . . . I will bet you not only that L'Amour will snatch you almost bodily into his story, but that he will give you an excellent thumbnail education . . ." The Los Angeles *Herald-Examiner* stated, "*The Walking Drum* is a truly rewarding labor of love that will appeal to L'Amour loyalists and strangers alike." The *Washington Post* called it, "a powerful book," and likened its appeal to "riding a rollercoaster with your arms up all the way." And the Los Angeles *Herald-Examiner* concluded, "above all,

L'Amour is the consummate storyteller . . . The novel is a fascinating epic adventure that will catch newcomers by surprise."

Such reviews must have helped smooth L'Amour's ruffled feathers. *Last of the Breed* did not fare as well, though the usually critical *Kirkus Review* declared, "for sheer adventure, L'Amour is in top form." And the Chicago *Sun-Times* predicted, "This book can't miss." Of course, *any* new novel by Louis L'Amour could not miss, at least in terms of sales. And despite the disappointing review of *The Haunted Mesa* in the *New York Times Book Review*, the Nashville *Banner* found that novel to be "vintage L'Amour."

But these are book reviews, which few people remember. Of the academic critics, perhaps John D. Nesbitt has best summarized the common critical consensus: "What the literary community seems to be responding to in L'Amour's fiction is a lack of depth in both vision and method. While the lean narratives of his early work have given way to more padded volumes beefed-up with pet paragraphs of philosophy and historical details, the story is essentially the same."

Nesbitt then goes on to describe what that recurrent L'Amour story most often is about: ". . . a physically superior white man fights his way unequivocally through adversity, wins a virtuous woman, settles conflicts with fist and gun, and becomes, decisively, a functioning member of civilization." L'Amour could protest all he liked that some people acted this way, Nesbitt concluded, but "the literary product is a repetitious story, vicarious problem-solving, and unambiguous conflict."

Many critics conclude that there is insufficient complexity in L'Amour's novels and stories, despite their growing length. Their designs and their characters' motivations seem simplistic. His much-touted heroes often are mere cardboard creations.

After taking it on the chin from the critics for so long, it must have given L'Amour enormous satisfaction when he was voted the National Gold Medal by the United States Congress, presented to him on September 24, 1983. The medal was personally handed to him by President Ronald Reagan, the former host of TV's "Death Valley Days." The medal, struck by the United States Mint, was voted to L'Amour "in recognition of his distinguished career as an author and his contributions to the nation through historically-based works."

In the history of the United States, the medal had been given to only 80 individuals. These include Thomas Alva Edison, Charles Lindberg, Marian Anderson, Irving Berlin, and Dr. Jonas Salk. Louis L'Amour was the first novelist ever to receive it. Robert Frost, the poet, had received the award earlier.

It probably did not hurt that President Reagan had publicly acknowledged appreciation of L'Amour's work. But bestowal of this particular medal is very heavily involved with politics of a non-partisan nature. "That's why so few people have gotten the award," according to Jack Evans, who began beating the drum on L'Amour's behalf, some time before.

It came about this way. Evans was a former California newspaperman who moved to Jamestown in 1969, where he assumed editorship of the *Jamestown Sun*, the town's daily paper, and of course began to hear tales about L'Amour. When L'Amour returned to Jamestown in 1972 to accept his Honorary Doctorate from the college, the two men met. Evans realized that the local favorite son deserved national recognition on the Presidential level. He began lobbying North Dakota's Congressional delegation. In 1978, he is said to personally have written, stamped, and mailed over three thousand letters at his own expense, in an attempt to influence individuals to support the idea of a medal for L'Amour.

Consequently, a bill was fairly well along in Congress in 1979. Then John Wayne died on June 11, 1979, and all sentiment went toward giving one to Wayne posthumously. The 1980 elections sidetracked yet another L'Amour bill. Then there was some horse-trading involved. The Michigan Congressional delegation pledged their support for L'Amour—if—North Dakota pledged their support for boxer Joe Louis, a Michigan native. Pennsylvania delegates pledged the same arrangement if North Dakota would support band leader Fred Waring, whose group had been known for decades as "The Pennsylvanians." As a result of such shenanigans, Congress voted medals to all three—L'Amour, Louis, and Waring—in August, 1982. The medals were officially bestowed at a White House ceremony in September of the following year.

President Reagan praised L'Amour's "enormous contributions to Western folklore and our frontier heritage." L'Amour is quoted in *Time* magazine as lamenting earlier that President Reagan had never starred in a film based on one of his novels. The novelist quipped, "Maybe I can talk him into doing one some day." A much later interview has L'Amour contemplating appearing in one of his films, himself.

Perhaps it would have been a good idea if he had. After *Hondo* and *Heller in Pink Tights*, films of L'Amour properties were pretty uninspired. Of Sam Wanamaker's 1971 production of *Catlow*, for instance, Roger Greenspan wrote in the *New York Times* that the film was not a coherent or even mildly pleasing movie: ". . . it ends up being about nothing at all, as if it were unaware of its own ideas or the potency of its images. And so tension becomes tedium and laughter grows tired and the screen recedes not quite out of sight, but surely out of mind."

Other films based on L'Amour's work which the novelist enjoyed were *Kid*

Rodelo, directed by Richard Carlson in 1966 (Carlson had directed *Four Guns to the Border* in 1954, as well) and *Shalako* (1968), directed by Edward Dmytryk, and which gave L'Amour his royal reception in London. *Shalako* has a cowboy in New Mexico in 1880 acting as a guide for a group of European aristocrats. The local Indians decide to attack the party. Despite occasional brutalities, the film never becomes very exciting. A far better film was *Taggart* (1965), directed by R.G. Springsteen from a script by Robert Creighton Williams. This L'Amour tale of revenge was made into a tight, tough adult Western.

"Adult western" is a term L'Amour would have sneered at. Around 1975, a new breed of Western arrived on the scene, escapades of cowpunchers whose romantic interests were by no means confined to their horses. Jake Logan, J.D. Hardin, and Zeke Masters are some of the authors of these X-rated oaters. Throughout his career, L'Amour never saw any need to open the bedroom door in his work.

In 1967-68 L'Amour broke into television. *Hondo* was made into an ABC television series. *Hondo* was a property that just wouldn't die; *Hondo and the Apaches* was a second theatrical release film, this one based on "The Gift of Cochise." It was directed by Lee H. Katzin, and was produced in 1967 by MGM.

In 1979 the Sackett saga became a TV miniseries, "The Sacketts", on NBC. It starred, among many others, Tom Selleck and Sam Elliott. L'Amour was reaching millions of additional fans through the TV screen. The TV series added a good deal to his wealth. Better yet, "The Sacketts" was voted the most authentic Western of the past decade by the Cowboy Hall of Fame of Oklahoma City. Ever a stickler for detail, L'Amour was gratified that historical detail had been observed meticulously in the big film of his saga.

CHAPTER FIVE

OLD AGE

It was 1983, and that summer a new aspect of Louis L'Amour's personality became public—his feistiness. He attempted to sue Carroll & Graf, a publisher who had announced the publication of two Louis L'Amour titles without seeking his permission.

What they had done was, rather enterprisingly, gathered early L'Amour stories from the pages of *Homicide Street* and

Rawhide Range. Due to carelessness on L'Amour's part, the copyright had expired and these stories fell into the public domain. While there is sometimes a gentleman's agreement in publishing that such material will not be used if the author is living and unwilling to have it published, there is nothing binding. L'Amour charged that Carroll & Graf had "deceived and misled" both the public and the booksellers by scheduling two books under his name, when he wasn't even aware of the books' contents.

The suit went back and forth. L'Amour sought a preliminary injunction and a temporary restraining order that would force the publisher to stop advertising and publishing the two books which had been announced for a September 1983 publication date. He also attempted to force the firm to reveal precisely which of his stories were included, in order for him to ascertain whether or not he held copyright to them.

Kent Carroll, publisher and executive editor of Carroll & Graf, retaliated that L'Amour's suit had "no merit whatsoever" and that all the stories were without the protection of copyright. "We're very comfortable with our position," he said in an interview in *Publishers Weekly*. "It's not our fault that the copyrights weren't renewed."

The two books were *The Hills of Homicide*, a collection of detective stories, as its title would indicate, and *Law of the Desert Born*, a collection of Western stories. L'Amour first heard of their existence from friends who attended the American Booksellers Association annual convention, held in Dallas in the spring of 1983. It was L'Amour's contention that Carroll & Graf "distributed deceptive, misleading and false promotional material" at the convention. The publishers went so far, he charged, as to indicate in some material that the two books were novels, were entirely new, and that L'Amour had authorized their publication.

Mr. Carroll claimed that his firm had been entirely "forthcoming and ethical" from the beginning. They offered to pay L'Amour royalties on both books, despite the fact there was no legal basis for their doing so. They solicited a short foreword or introduction to the books as well; L'Amour said "No" to both offers. All he wanted, apparently, was a list of titles to be included. Carroll assumed this was in order to allow L'Amour to rush the list to Bantam, his long-time publisher, so they might quickly bring out their editions of the two collections and pre-empt the market.

In a final attempt at negotiation, Carroll & Graf offered to tell L'Amour the titles of all the stories to be published in both books —if—he kept the list confidential and did not share it with Bantam Books. This offer also was icily rejected.

After some heated hearings, Carroll & Graf were declared free and clear to publish the two books. They were, however, ordered to change some of their advertising and promotion, as well as the books' covers. Somehow, L'Amour foxily determined what stories were being reprinted on his own, and he got Bantam Books to crank into overtime, producing what L'Amour proclaimed to be "The Only Authorized Editions." That claim appeared in a special seal bearing his photo on the cover of both Bantam books, with the additional—and somewhat misleading—claim, "First Time in Paperback."

In a Foreword, L'Amour made no mention of the profit motive. Instead, he claimed the Bantam editions were issued "To offer my readers the chance to have the proper presentation of these stories ..." L'Amour did add introductory historical notes that precede each story and a few additional stories, making the Bantam editions potentially more desirable than the Carroll & Graf editions. "Only accept short story collections with my name on them that are published by Bantam," he commanded his readers. It gratified L'Amour that the Bantam editions far outsold the "unauthorized" ones. L'Amour was so outraged by the Carroll & Graf episode that he publicly announced he would never autograph one copy of the offending books. As far as he was concerned, they did not even exist.

But Carroll & Graf may have had the last word. Two-and-a-half years later, they published similarly "unauthorized" versions of two more story collections, *Riding for the Brand* and *Dutchman's Flat*. Once more, L'Amour and Bantam had to burn the midnight oil to rush out authorized editions of the same material—or basically the same material. L'Amour even attempted to lay a guilt trip upon the public by stating he had had to put aside the new novel he was working on, in order to select and edit the stories and prepare the introductory notes. If he did indeed postpone work on a novel, it could not have been for long. In 1986 he published his 95th novel, *Last of the Breed*, which Bantam issued initially as a $17.95 hardback. L'Amour was becoming gentrified.

By now, L'Amour had accumulated a great deal of wealth, and his books were copyrighted by "Louis L'Amour Enterprises." Besides the hardcovers, paperbacks, translations, films and TV series, in recent years Louis L'Amour had become a cottage industry. Not only were all the books in print, but within the books themselves there were special offers: for Louis L'Amour audio cassettes, on which the master introduces and reads his short stories; for special hardcover "Heritage Editions" of the novels—available in regular or special leather bindings; for a Louis L'Amour Sweepstakes; for a special Silver Anniversary Celebration of *The*

Sacketts; for his daughter's forthcoming anthology of his wit and wisdom; and even, offers for L'Amour's forthcoming guide to the Sacketts—coming just in time for Christmas gift-giving. In addition, ads for L'Amour short-story collections contained checklists with little boxes, so readers could tick-off those they had not yet read (or bought).

One thing L'Amour was doing with his money was investing in real estate. In addition to the house in Bel-Air, he owned a ranch in Bakersfield, California. He was a great believer in capitalism. He never once doubted his ability, not only to succeed, but to prevail. This was perhaps over-compensation for the trauma he suffered when his father went flat broke during the Depression, and he felt compelled to break loose and make it on his own. With great bravura, he told one interviewer, "If I weren't a writer, I could see *dozens* of ways that I could be a millionaire in a short time. Starting right from where I am or starting from scratch—either one. This is a time when the idea is the thing. Nothing is closed off; the opportunities are different from what they used to be, that's all. Self-made men are still possible." In the year of publication of *The Walking Drum*, he bought a 1,000-acre ranch near Durango, Colorado. It was his intention to live part of every year there— to absorb atmosphere and color. His ranch looks out upon a valley watered by the Animas River, which the Spaniards called El Rio de las Animas—the river of lost souls. The barn and the granary have been on his property for over 100 years. His ranch house, which he and Kathy remodeled, is of the same vintage. The author, ever curious about the past, managed to determine that his ranch was directly on the route followed by the Franciscan friar, Silvestre-Vélez de Escalante. Over 200 years earlier the friar had made his way from Santa Fe through the Rockies and into Utah. L'Amour even had the exact date he said the friar passed by his ranch—August 8, 1776.

Then there is his other big real estate project which he hoped to see to completion. This is a multi-million dollar land investment in Colorado, some eleven miles west of Durango. It was his intention to establish an authentic Western town of the

1865-1886 vintage. It would be a tourist attraction, such as Colonial Williamsburg or Old Sturbridge, only everything there would be authentically frontier. The town would also be used as a location for filming Western movies and TV shows.

The town was to be called "Shalako", after his fictional hero, Shalako Carlin. News stories about this project appeared from time to time. L'Amour pointed out there was still an old narrow-gauge railway to the town. He boasted of "already getting applications from all over the world from people who want to work there." And in Bantam Books' publicity releases, there were descriptions of Shalako: "Historically accurate from whistle to well, it will be a live, operating town."

It was to be built with funds from L'Amour's own corporation, Shalako Enterprises. A cost was estimated to be some $30,000,000, and the site was estimated from 1,000 to 2,000 acres on Highway 160. The town's attractions would include saloons, a general store, a coal mine, a gold mine, a jail, doctors' and lawyers' offices, a hotel, a livery stable, a school—everything authentic, complete with the absence of plumbing and electricity, according to an article in *North Dakota Motorist*.

But something happened to prevent completion of his dream and potential investment. Later Bantam blurbs, when mentioning Shalako at all, reported it would be authentic, "when it is constructed." More recent "About the Author" blurbs, fail to mention the project at all.

According to Robert L. Gale, utility companies and environmentalists are causing the delays in construction. If so, this would be highly ironic, considering how very respectful of the environment L'Amour was all his life, as well as in his work. By writing as he did of ecological concerns—and reaching millions upon millions of readers—there is every probability his influence improved the environment.

As he wrote in *The Lonesome Gods*, ". . . we must never forget that the land and the waters are ours for the moment only, that generations will follow who must themselves live from that land and drink that water. It would not be enough to leave something for them; we must leave it all a little better than we found it." The book from which this quotation comes remained on the *Publishers Weekly* hardback best-seller list for nineteen weeks consecutively in 1983. That was the same year Louis L'Amour sneaked up behind President Reagan like Chick Bowdrie, to receive his Congressional Gold Medal. The medal bore the lines from *To the Far Blue Mountain* which are the epigraph to this book. It also bore a remarkable likeness of L'Amour, wearing the inevitable ten-gallon hat.

The very next year, with what must have been a feeling of *déjà vu*, Louis L'Amour was awarded what was to be his greatest honor, the United States Government Medal of Freedom. It was presented, again, by President Reagan at the White House. L'Amour returned a second time to the place where his ancestor, General Henry Dearborn, was entertained by President Jefferson. The date of L'Amour's high honor was March 26, 1984. On that day, he received the United States' Government's highest civilian award.

President Reagan hailed L'Amour for "having brought the West to the people of the East and to people everywhere." After the ceremony, President and Nancy Reagan met with the recipients in the East Room. The Medal of Freedom recipients that year, besides L'Amour, were Senator Howard R. Baker, Jr.; Whittaker Chambers, editor (awarded posthumously); Les Charne, economist; Dr. Denton Cooley, heart surgeon; Tennessee Ernie Ford, entertainer; Dr. Hector Garcia, founder of the Mexican-American equal rights group; General Andrew Goodpaste, former NATO Commander; Eunice Kennedy Shriver; Lincoln Kirstein, ballet entrepreneur and poet; President Anwar ei-Sadat of Egypt (awarded posthumously); James Cagney, actor; and Norman Vincent Peale, clergyman. During the festivities L'Amour was again heard to say he hoped to appear in a film made from one of his properties.

Later that year, L'Amour was given his second honorary Doctorate degree—this one from Pepperdine University in California.

During his golden years, L'Amour became somewhat of a cultural and literary philanthropist—though he would have bridled at that word. He was a member of the executive council of the Center for the Book within the Library of Congress. L'Amour was proud of that particular affiliation. He felt books were being forgotten. "In an electronic world there's a question whether people will still read ... My education from books didn't depend upon a power source." He appeared on the "Great Teachers" television show. He was a member of the Academy of Motion Picture Arts and Sciences, as well as the California Academy of Sciences. And he continued to encourage painter Clifford Brycelea.

He also sponsored a number of outstanding high school students who were honored annually by the American Academy of Achievement, based in California. The Academy would bring in teenagers of unusual scholastic achievement, where they would attend three-day seminars with nationally-known figures, such as Nobel and Pulitzer Prize winners.

Another of L'Amour's pet projects involved books. It was to be a "Library of Americana." The site was not yet settled upon, although at one time it was felt it might be located on his own ranch. In either event, it was to be somewhere in the Four

Corners region of the West, where four states meet contiguously: Utah, Colorado, Arizona and New Mexico.

As L'Amour explained the project to *Smithsonian* magazine, "The idea is to assemble local publications from all around America—memoirs, local histories, historical society booklets, newspaper pamphlets—there are thousands of them. It's history that the historians never see. I'd include the basic books on American history and the historical and genealogical manuscripts that readers send me."

For years, his mail contained Western journals and diaries, family archives, genealogical records, and the like, that people found in their attics and barns and thoughtfully passed on to L'Amour, as one who would make better use of them. Sometimes they were simply addressed to:

LOUIS L'AMOUR,
AUTHOR,
LOS ANGELES, CAL.

The letters and packages were always delivered.

What L'Amour envisioned was an enormous national archive where responsible scholars could study American history as told by ordinary individuals who, in most cases, lived the events described, rather than history as regurgitated by scholars from books. In 1987, he expressed hope that the archive would be completed and in operation within five years. Today its fate is uncertain.

When *The Haunted Mesa* was published in the summer of 1987, it, too, was reviewed in the *New York Times Book Review*. The reviewer this time was Jack Sullivan. He concluded that, "as always, Mr. L'Amour is adept at tight plotting, meticulous re-search, and authoritative sense of place." But he went on to say that the writing was tired and lacked the energy of the best L'Amour westerns.

No doubt L'Amour *was* tired. He had published 102 books by then—86 novels, 14 short-story collections, 1 full-length book of nonfiction, and his early book of poems. He had placed about four-hundred short stories in some eighty magazines, both here and abroad. Many of those books were researched first-hand, by scouting the terri-tory, and through reading. He had written numerous film scripts and about sixty-five television scripts. More than forty of his titles had been made into films. There were almost 200 million copies of his books in circulation. All but the book of poems were still in print.

Tired or not, it did appear L'Amour would go on forever. That was his constitution.

After *The Haunted Mesa*, he completed a Western short story collection to be titled *Lonigan*. He also finished *The Sackett Companion*, a nonfiction book rehearsing all the facts and research that went into his popular 17-novel saga. He intended the book as a commentary to accompany the series, an aid to the reader, and just possibly as a boost to his reputation as a scholar and serious producer of literature. It is scheduled to appear in the stores in time for Christmas gift-giving in 1988.

And there were other projects on his desk. There was a frontier novel, tentatively titled *South Pass*. He was writing a nonfiction book about the history of Cordoba, Spain. He also planned another nonfiction volume on the trade, travel, and cultural diffusion of Asia. To this project he had given the beautiful title, *Sandalwood, Cedarwood, and Sweet White Wine*.

Still another ambitious project was to be a trilogy on a Cheyenne Indian from his birth to his death. "He won't see a white man until the last page of the first book," L'Amour promised. He was determined to show exactly how the Indians lived. Part of the plot revolved around how this Indian discovered the horse for the first time, and what an enormous difference it made to his life. After his encounter with the horse and his first white man, the character will then become involved in the Indian wars.

Yet another project was an encyclopedic collection of odd facts about the West, which L'Amour had been encountering all his life. It would, he reckoned, run to well over 1000 pages.

Then there were the remaining two volumes of his 12th-century European and Asian saga. We know that L'Amour had delayed the writing of the second volume. In "A Message from Louis L'Amour" tucked in the back of the paperback edition of *The Walking Drum*, he reported he had completed much of the research for the second volume, but not the writing. He stated that many readers had written to say how eager they were to find out what happens to Kerbouchard, the hero of volume one, when he follows Sundari to what is today called India. L'Amour assured his readers that no one was more eager to follow Kerbouchard than he—but his next historical novel had to be *Jubal Sackett*, the eighteenth novel in that saga, which he had postponed writing for some time. It was published in 1985. Whether or not L'Amour then returned to Kerbouchard's adventures is a matter of conjecture.

Despite earlier protestations that he could not write such a book, it also appears that he had gotten around to writing his autobiography.

And in the press, he had teased about outer space being the last frontier: "We are a pioneer people still. If I believed in predestination, I'd say we had been specially chosen for the purpose of going out in space . . . It's something buried in our genes." He predicted space colonies and intergalactic expeditions, as if Mars were just another mesa.

Like the protagonist in Robert Frost's

famous poem, Louis L'Amour "had miles to go before I sleep."

L'Amour relished what he did, and even the time he did it in. "People ask me what is the best time to be alive," he once said. "I tell them that *this* is the best time. People think this is a bad time. It isn't at all. We have a greater variety of food available today than ever before. The average poor man today eats better than a king did 150 years ago."

"Nope," he said, examining the four-color portrait of himself on the back of a recent paperback edition of one of his novels. "I wouldn't change a thing."

EPILOGUE

It was a stunned public that learned, on Monday, June 13, 1988, that Louis L'Amour had died at his home on Friday, June 10. He was eighty years old. The family had delayed the announcement by a day or two in order that they could personally inform L'Amour's friends of his death. They did not want his close associates to hear it on the radio, or to read it in the newspaper.

The cause of death was listed as lung cancer—an odd fate inasmuch as he had never smoked in his life, according to Stuart S. Applebaum, his editor. L'Amour's doctor suggested the cancer originated in the writer's days as a miner. But L'Amour did not hold with that theory. Earlier he had written that he'd worked in all sorts of mines—but never a coal mine.

He was a stoical man. He had written in *Treasure Mountain*, "Death never spent time in my thoughts, for where a man is, there is no death . . ." And from his writing one can assume he believed in an afterlife. In *Conagher*, for instance, one encounters this passage: "I figure it's like the Plains Indians say—a happy hunting ground. Leastways, that's how I'd like it to be. A place with mountains, springs, running streams, and some green, grassy banks where a man can lie with hat over his eyes and let the bees buzz."

Joseph Wershba, a TV news producer based in Manhattan who had known L'Amour for over a decade, summed up the nation's disbelief in L'Amour's demise: "He and John Wayne were cut from the same mold, the kind that doesn't complain . . . I had thought he'd go easily to 95 with all his powers intact ... still turning out books." (John Wayne, The Duke, had died of lung cancer a few years before, and Geraldine Page just the year before. So now the author and both stars of *Hondo* were history.) Film producer Saul David, once L'Amour's editor, and perhaps even responsible for his discovery, called L'Amour "the only moveable piece of Mt. Rushmore."

He died with his boots on. In the last hours of his life he was said to be proofreading the typescript of his autobiography, to be called *Education of a Wandering Man*. This is only appropriate. In *The Lonesome Gods*, he had mused, "If man is to vanish from the earth, let him vanish in the moment of creation, when he is creating something new ... It is man's nature to reach out, to grasp for the tangible on the way to the intangible." He also lived to see a copy of Angelique's Father's Day present for him, her anthology of quotations from his books, *A Trail of Memories*.

The funeral was private, a quiet end for one of the world's most popular writers, and a man who had been presented to a Princess and honored by a President. Just the week before, former President Jimmy Carter had been reading *The Lonesome Gods* on an airplane trip. President Reagan had read *Jubal Sackett* while recovering from his much-publicized surgery for cancer in 1985. President Dwight David Eisenhower had passed his well-thumbed copies along to Secret Service men. Tom Landry packs a L'Amour along with his Dallas Cowboys playbook whenever he goes on the road. Other fans included Israeli Defense Minister Ezer Weizman and country star Willie Nelson. L'Amour himself had stated he loved to fly, because then he could look down at all the houses and know that, in many of them, right then, someone was reading his books.

Louis L'Amour led quite a life. From his humble beginnings in the Dakotas, to his knock-about youth with exotic jobs and many ocean crossings, to a global war followed by fame and celebrity and wealth —he never stopped the momentum. He became, as *Time* magazine dubbed him, "a kind of Woody Guthrie of fiction," a conservative populist who created myths and believed the myths he created. His fans could not wait for the next L'Amour to hit the racks; they by-passed the centerfold magazines in order to buy them. And he worked hard not to disappoint them.

His audience was very important to him. He tried to answer every fan letter he received—and in some years he received 5,000. He said he was careful, in his books, never to write down to his audience. To do so, he felt, would be insulting to them. "Nearly every question in every letter I've received has an intelligent comment to make or an intelligent question to ask," he told Michael T. Marsden. Once he was on a radio show in Houston, Texas, for three consecutive hours, and the switchboard was constantly lit up with people calling in to ask L'Amour questions. The questions they asked showed an insatiable need to know details about the Frontier. How much would a covered wagon carry, and how much would it weigh? Why did the pioneers use oxen instead of mules or horses? L'Amour's answers were knowledgeable and often surprising. In response to the latter, for instance, he said oxen were used because their hooves spread on turf and can walk better on turf than horses or mules. Secondly, the oxen were better eating than horsemeat or mule meat, in case the pioneers were forced to use them for food!

L'Amour's writing was not high art, but it was high entertainment. His was the voice at the side of the campfire, or the voice at the end of the bar, telling a story and telling it so well, one can't bear not to hear how the story ends. *People* magazine described him as the kind of writer who "makes the wolves come out of the woods to listen." He fed our illusions, our cravings for adventure. In *Shalako* he summed up the lure of the West: "A man in the Western lands was as big or as bad as he wished."

Marc Jaffe, Bantam's editorial director, would agree: "We've been through Watergate, Vietnam, and other crises in which it was hard to separate good from evil ... Now we're searching for simple, eternal verities. In L'Amour's books, the good guy is a good guy and the bad guy is a bad guy. Readers want that. They're searching for truth, courage, success in overcoming serious odds."[7]

7. *Wall Street Journal*, Jan. 19, 1978

Ray Walters, writing in the *New York Times Book Review* in 1980, offered another theory for the success of L'Amour and other Western writers: "Now that the nation is in a time of trial . . . Americans are taking a renewed interest and pride in their past." It is possible that L'Amour's plots, with their violence necessary for survival, was reassuring to a country which had lived through Viet Nam, Cuba, the Dominican Republic, Chile, and El Salvador. Tom Sullivan pushes this theory to the extreme when he mused in the pages of the *Southwest Review*, "One wonders how many of those planning a 'survivable' nuclear war have one of the various Sackett family sagas at their bedside for innocent bedtime reading."

Today, the market for Westerns is dwindling somewhat. But L'Amour's sales keep climbing. He alone accounts for about half the market. The major reason L'Amour is read is because of his authenticity. His close attention to detail makes his work ring true. He walked the land he wrote about, had known his subjects better than most.

"A lot of things I know about the West,"

he told one interviewer, "I don't think anybody else knew. I've had the opportunity of being on the ground and talking with a lot of people who participated in it. I think I'm the last writer who'll have that chance."

He had a point. Few writers of Westerns knew the territory and the people as well as L'Amour. From his Indian friendships to his outlaw acquaintances, he experienced the real thing. His background was quite a contrast to that of Zane Grey, perhaps the next most famous writer of Westerns. Before he began writing, Grey was a dentist in New York City! And Max Brand—i.e., one Frederick Faust—when sent out West to soak up atmosphere, holed himself up in his motel room and read Medieval literature.

And it wasn't just the West L'Amour knew and researched meticulously—it was everything, from the Far Eastern costumes in *The Walking Drum*—he possessed twenty books on costume alone—to the lingo of the underworld in *The Hills of Homicide*. In the pages of the latter, the reader encounters words such as "shiv" and "torpedos" and "punch jobs"—an entire criminal language. L'Amour actually had friends on the police force get him interviews with a large number of men and women who had spent time in the penitentiary. Once, when he was researching what he called the "economies of crime," he interviewed a bunch of thugs whose speciality was grand larceny.

Given his enormous productivity, if one had to choose the essential Louis L'Amour work, what should one read? This is a difficult question, because once one gets addicted, one wants more L'Amour. Many are willing to read the slow-moving with the swift, not to miss out on any.

The general critical consensus would be that his short stories are not as good as his novels. And among the scores of novels, three stand out: *Hondo*, *Flint*, and *Bendigo Shafter*. But the first novel L'Amour claimed under his own name, *Westward the Tide*, is also suspenseful and well organized. And its historical background remains background rather than the subject of a sermon on the butte. *Hondo* is L'Amour's most famous novel, and for reasons other than having been a John Wayne film. Its plot is simple and easy to follow. There aren't eighty characters to keep separate in one's head. In fact, much of the action involves the interaction between only two characters, Hondo—the outwardly driven male principle, and Angie—the inwardly driven female principle. As Marsden, one of L'Amour's best critics, has observed, their "Omega point" is "hearth and home, the end of all Westward Movement."

Flint is a thrilling novel about a New Mexico gunman. In it, L'Amour displays some of his insider's knowledge of boxing. As mentioned earlier, along with *Hondo* it was rated one of the twenty-five best Western novels. And *Bendigo Shafter* deserves to be mentioned in the same breath with both. It is a first-person narrative of over 300 pages, and covers Bendigo's youth, young manhood, and maturity. L'Amour's sympathy for the Native American is nowhere more apparent than in his characterization of Uruwishi, an old warrior who is the most admirable person in the book. Robert L. Gale has called this novel "a major work and a first-rate piece of fiction—clearly one of the four or five most important books thus far in L'Amour's career." L'Amour published nothing after Gale's assessment to change that opinion.

That still leaves over 95 books to contend with! Among those, the following stand out: *The Burning Hills* features one of L'Amour's few Hispanic characters, and is a successful and uncomplicated tale of revenge. It is also highly suspenseful, because—like *Jubal Sackett*—the novel begins in the middle of the plot and works its way backward.

Two of L'Amour's best books on the second tier were both published in 1957: *Sitka* and *Last Stand at Papago Wells*. *Sitka* is one of his best-organized novels, yet is longer than any of the books which preceded it. The plot revolves about the Alaska Purchase, "Seward's Folly," and real historical figures mingle with the fictional, as in Gore Vidal's historical novels. The fictional hero, Jean LaBarge, is one of L'Amour's most fully developed, and compared favorably in his complexity with Kerbouchard of *The Walking Drum*. *Last Stand at Papago Wells* is also well-constructed. It is one of the first of many novels in which L'Amour will have a white orphan pursued by a group of Indians. The writing reflects the level L'Amour could achieve when he wasn't bound to producing three books a year.

How the West Was Won, discussed earlier, is a L'Amour novel of epic proportions covering four generations on the frontier. Its five bulky sections are named "The River," "The Plains," "The War," "The Iron Horse," and "The Outlaws." The action seems to move along non-stop.

The first of L'Amour's books to be set in the twentieth century was *The Broken Gun*. In that sense, it represents a breakthrough. Both *Last of the Breed* and *The Haunted Mesa* are also set in this century. Very much so, in fact. Aircraft figure in the former, and in the latter the Navajos travel by pickup truck. *The Broken Gun* does not follow a familiar formula, and might be one of his more autobiographical books.

Down the Long Hills already has been discussed briefly as worthy of the award it was given. As Gale remarks, for a L'Amour novel it "is remarkably unified in time, place and action."

For a plot that surprises the reader on every turn, *Callaghen* is recommended. The book also boasts some broad humor of the Western tall-tale variety. It is distinguished from other L'Amour novels in that it is an army novel. Mort Callaghen, with his soldier-of-fortune past, may be modeled upon an individual L'Amour met in the Far East. If so, he put him in a time machine and shot him back to frontier days.

If you like detective stories, you should try *Borden Chantry*. It's a Western, all right, but the author used his knowledge of the detective trade to tell his tale. Like the later *The Iron Marshall* and *Milo Talon*, the plot involves the accumulation of clues in order to solve a murder. L'Amour doesn't out-Sherlock Holmes, but the result is pleasing all the same.

On the other hand, if your taste runs to swashbucklers, there is *Fair Blows the Wind*. It falls within the Chantry series, takes place roughly between 1573 and 1590, and is a real page-turner.

If you have feminist leanings, on the other hand, you'll appreciate what L'Amour accomplishes in *The Cherokee Trail*. Here his leading protagonist is a woman, and seems to constitute his women's liberation statement. Opposing all odds, Mary Breyton holds her own in a man's world—without a man.

One of L'Amour's longest novels—yet one of his most carefully written—is *The Lone-*

some Gods. In one interview, he stated he had conceived of the work twenty years before it was published. All that rumination on the plot and character show. As in so many of the novels, the hero is a young man out on his own, learning from nature as well as from books, learning how to fight and survive, even in the desert. *The Lonesome Gods* is obviously one of L'Amour's most autobiographical books. Taken with *The Broken Gun*, and the nonfiction *Frontier*, one might feel he knows a lot more about the man behind the typewriter. And once again, there is a friendly Indian on hand to help the young protagonist in his times of need.

Of the Sackett novels, *Jubal Sackett* is the most satisfying all around. Others that reward the reader are *Sackett Brand*, *Sackett's Land*, *To the Blue Mountains*, *Day Breakers*, and *Ride the Dark Trail*. Others in the series, less effective and more diffuse, are also less believable.

Of his three late blockbusters, *The Walking Drum*, *Last of the Breed*, and *The Haunted Mesa*, the latter—with its delving into magic and the supernatural—casts a spell unique in the L'Amour canon. All three, however, are repetitive and not really among his most gripping novels.

And what of the short-story collections? The two Chick Bowdrie books—*Bowdrie* and *Bowdrie's Law*—are the most solid, though portions of *Yondering* are worth reading for the light they shed directly and indirectly upon L'Amour's vagabond years. Many of the salty characters one meets are equal to the rawhide men of the novels.

Lastly, *Frontier*—his only non-fiction book—is essential reading for L'Amour fans. The photos are breathtaking, and the prose concise and to the point; one suspects this book actually was edited.

So much for L'Amour at his best. If you're interested in investigating his least distinguished writing, check out *Fallon*, a cardsharp novel which he must have written in about ten minutes back in 1963. One would think it a parody of L'Amour if one did not know better. Parodies aren't tedious. One gets the feeling that no editor at any time said, "Louis, this isn't good enough, try again." Or, "Forget this book, go on to your next."

But preferences, as always, are individual matters. One can meet readers who have read every single Louis L'Amour title and loved them all. One thing is for sure: Despite his forays into the detective story, the espionage novel, the swashbuckler and the supernatural, it is the Western for which he will be remembered. Louis L'Amour charted the desires of Americans in the heartland. He affirmed their values of hard work, family life, friendship, honor, justice, loyalty, and even dreaming. He was our Professor Emeritus of Western folklore. He devoted his lifetime to separating fact from fancy. He showed us the West as it really was, demythologized. And more than any other writer, he made the Western novel a national pastime.

It was a life of unusual dedication. The typewriter was heard at his house seven days a week for decades. The only exception was when he was traveling to scout locations for stories. But Louis L'Amour would not have had it any other way. "I work all the time," he said in 1976. "I love it and can't stay away from it. I am a man intoxicated with my country and its people. If I had a thousand years, I could not tell the stories, nor put into words, half of what I feel."

To paraphrase a passage from his own *The Lonely Men*, L'Amour succeeded in putting words upon paper, as he was driven to do, and also wrote large upon the page of life that was left open for him.

* * * * *

BIBLIOGRAPHY
AND
CHECKLISTS

A LOUIS L'AMOUR CHECKLIST

Primary Sources

A. Poetry Collection

Smoke from This Altar. Oklahoma City: Lusk Publishing Co., 1939

B. Non-Fiction Collections

Frontier. With photographs by David Muench. New York: Bantam Books, 1984

A Trail of Memories. The Quotations of Louis L'Amour. Compiled by Angelique L'Amour. New York: Bantam Books, 1988

The Sackett Companion. New York: Bantam Books, 1988

C. Story Collections

War Party. New York: Bantam Books, 1975; 1987

The Strong Shall Live. New York: Bantam Books, 1980; 1987

Yondering. New York: Bantam Books, 1980; 1988

Buckskin Run. New York: Bantam Books, 1981

Bowdrie. New York: Bantam Books, 1983

The Hills of Homicide. New York: Bantam Books, 1983; New York: Carroll & Graf, 1983

Law of the Desert Born. New York: Carroll & Graf, 1983; New York: Bantam Books, 1984

Bowdrie's Law. New York: Bantam Books, 1984; 1985

Riding for the Brand. New York: Carroll &

Graf, 1986; New York: Bantam Books, 1986

Dutchman's Flat. New York: Bantam Books, 1986; New York: Carroll & Graf, 1986

Night Over the Solomons. New York: Bantam Books, 1986

The Trail to Crazy Man. New York: Bantam Books, 1986

Lonigan. New York: Bantam Books, 1988

D. Novels

Hopalong Cassidy and the Riders of High Rock (as Tex Burns). New York: Doubleday, 1951

Hopalong Cassidy and the Rustlers of West Fork (as Tex Burns). New York: Doubleday, 1951

Hopalong Cassidy and the Trail to Seven Pines (as Tex Burns). New York: Doubleday, 1952

Hopalong Cassidy, Trouble Shooter (as Tex Burns). New York: Doubleday, 1953

Westward the Tide. London: World Works, 1950; 1977

Hondo. Greenwich, Conn: Fawcett, 1953; 1983; 1987

Showdown at Yellow Butte (as Jim Mayo). New York: Ace, 1953; 1983; 1987

Crossfire Trail. New York: Ace, 1953; 1983; 1987

Kilkenny. New York: Ace, 1954; 1983

Utah Blaine (as Jim Mayo). New York: Ace, 1954; 1982; 1986

Guns of the Timberlands. New York: Jason Press, 1955; 1985

Heller with a Gun. Greenwich, Conn: Fawcett, 1955; 1984; 1985

To Tame a Land. Greenwich, Conn: Fawcett, 1955; 1984; 1987

The Burning Hills. New York: Jason Press, 1956; 1985

Silver Canyon. New York: Avalon, 1956; 1987

Sitka. New York: Appleton, Century Crofts, 1957; 1958; 1986

Last Stand at Papago Wells. Greenwich, Conn.: Fawcett, 1957; 1985; 1986

The Tall Stranger. Greenwich, Conn.: Fawcett, 1957; 1986

Radigan. New York: Bantam Books, 1958; 1986

The First Fast Draw. New York: Bantam Books, 1959; 1976

Taggart. New York: Bantam Books, 1959; 1987

Day Breakers. New York: Bantam Books, 1960; 1967

Flint. New York: Bantam Books, 1960; 1975

Sackett. New York: Bantam Books, 1961; 1977

Shalako. New York: Bantam Books, 1962; 1985

Killoe. New York: Bantam Books, 1962; 1985; 1986

High Lonesome. New York: Bantam Books, 1962; 1971; 1985

Fallon. New York: Bantam Books, 1963; 1981

How the West Was Won. New York: Bantam Books, 1963

Catlow. New York: Bantam Books, 1963; 1975

Dark Canyon. New York: Bantam Books, 1963

Mojave Crossing. New York: Bantam Books, 1964

Hanging Woman Creek. New York: Bantam Books, 1964; 1987

Kiowa Trail. New York: Bantam Books, 1964; 1980

Highgraders. New York: Bantam Books, 1965; 1975

Sackett Brand. New York: Bantam Books, 1965; 1985

Key-Lock Man. New York: Bantam Books, 1965; 1986

Broken Gun. New York: Bantam Books, 1966; 1984

Kid Rodelo. New York: Bantam Books, 1966; 1986

Mustang Man. New York: Bantam Books, 1966; 1986

Kilrone. New York: Bantam Books, 1966; 1985

Skyliners. New York: Bantam Books, 1967; 1972

Matagorda. New York: Bantam Books, 1967

Down the Long Hills. New York: Bantam Books, 1968; 1978

Chancy. New York: Bantam Books, 1968; 1984

Brionne. New York: Bantam Books, 1968; 1981

The Empty Land. New York: Bantam Books, 1969; 1985

The Lonely Men. New York: Bantam Books, 1969; 1985

Conagher. New York: Bantam Books, 1969; 1987

The Man Called Noon. New York: Bantam Books, 1971; 1985

Galloway. New York: Bantam Books, 1970; 1986

Reilly's Luck. New York: Bantam Books, 1970; 1982

North to the Rails. New York: Bantam Books, 1971; 1987

Under the Sweetwater Rim. New York: Bantam Books, 1971; 1979

Tucker. New York: Bantam Books, 1971; 1981

Callaghen. New York: Bantam Books, 1972; 1985

Ride the Dark Trail. New York: Bantam Books, 1972; 1986

Treasure Mountain. New York: Bantam Books, 1972; 1986

The Ferguson Rifle. New York: Bantam Books, 1973

The Man from Skibbereen. New York: Bantam Books, 1973; 1987

The Quick and the Dead. New York: Bantam Books, 1973; 1979

The Californios. New York: Saturday Review Press, 1974; 1986

Sackett's Land. New York: Saturday Review Press, 1974; 1975

Rivers West. New York: Saturday Review Press, 1975; 1987

The Man from the Broken Hills. New York: Bantam Books, 1975

Over on the Dry Side. New York: Saturday Review Press, 1975; 1976; 1988

The Rider of Lost Creek. New York: Bantam Books, 1976; 1986

To the Far Blue Mountains. New York: Saturday Review Press, 1976; 1977

Where the Long Grass Blows. New York: Bantam Books, 1976; 1988

Borden Chantry. New York: Bantam Books, 1977

Fair Blows the Wind. New York: E.P. Dutton, 1978

The Mountain Valley War. New York: Bantam Books, 1978; 1982

Bendigo Shafter. New York: E.P. Dutton, 1979; 1987

The Proving Trail. New York: Bantam Books, 1979

The Iron Marshall. New York: Bantam Books, 1979; 1987

The Warrior's Path. New York: Bantam Books, 1980

Lonely on the Mountain. New York: Bantam Books, 1980; 1986

Comstock Lode. New York: Bantam Books, 1981; 1982

Milo Talon. New York: Bantam Books, 1981; 1986; 1987

The Tall Stranger. Greenwich: Fawcett Books, 1982; 1986

The Cherokee Trail. New York: Bantam Books, 1982

The Shadow Riders. New York: Bantam Books, 1982

The Lonesome Gods. New York: Bantam Books, 1983

Ride the River. New York: Bantam Books, 1983

Son of a Wanted Man. New York: Bantam Books, 1984

The Walking Drum. New York: Bantam Books, 1984; G.K. Hall, 1984

Jubal Sackett. New York: Bantam Books, 1985

Last of the Breed. New York: Bantam Books, 1986

The Haunted Mesa. New York: Bantam Books, 1987

E. Uncollected Writings

"An Open Letter to the Old Buckaroos," *Roundup*, 11 (Sept.-Oct., 1963), 2, 4-5

"Forewords to *The Sackett Novels* of Louis L'Amour," 4 Vols. 1980: 1: vii-ix; 2: vii-x; 3: vii-viii; 4: vii-viii

"Letter to Wesley Laing, 14 September, 1979". In *Kilkenny*, ed. Wesley Laing (Boston: Gregg Press, 1980), xi.

"The West of the Story," *Writer's Digest*, 60 (Dec. 1980), 27-29

"The West—The Greatest Story Ever Told." *Roundup*, 29 (July-Aug., 1981), 4-7

"Books in Their Saddlebags: The Men Who Made the Trail." *American West*, 19 (July-Aug., 1982), 46-47, 68

"Of Guns & Gunmen." *Gun World*, 25 (Sept. 1984), 54-56

F. Unpublished Screenplays

East of Sumatra. With Frank J. Gill, Jr. and Jack Natteford, 1953

Four Guns to the Border. With George Van Marter and Franklin Coen, 1954

Treasure of the Ruby Hills. With Tom Hubbard and Fred Eggers, 1955

Stranger on Horseback. With Herb Meadow and Don Martin, 1955

Kid Rodelo. With Jack Natteford, 1966

G. Secondary Sources

Anon. "L'Amour, Louis (Dearborn)," *Current Biography*, 1980. New York: H.W. Wilson, 203-206

_____. "L'Amour, Louis (Dearborn), 1908-," *Contemporary Authors*, New Revision Series, Vol. 3. Detroit: Gale Publishers, 322-323

_____. *Authors in the News*, Vol. 2, 1976

_____. "Medal of Freedom Recipients," *New York Times*, March 27, 1984, A25

_____. Review of *Bendigo Shafter*, *Publishers' Weekly*, Nov. 27, 1978, 49

_____. "The Undisputed King of Paperback Westerns," *San Francisco Chronicle*, Jan. 22, 1975, 16

Bannon, Barbara A. "Louis L'Amour," *Publishers' Weekly*, Oct. 8, 1973, 56-57

Barron, James. "Louis L'Amour, Writer, Is Dead," *New York Times*, June 13, 1988, D12

Bloodworth, William A. Review of *Fair Blows the Wind*. *Western American Literature*, 13 (Winter 1979), 365-66

Bulow, Ernest L. "Still Tall in the Saddle; Louis L'Amour's Classic Western Hero," *The Possible Sack*, June-July 1972, 1-8

Campbell, Charles. "Surging Seventies: Oklahoma Writers Published in 1970-71-72-73," Oklahoma Department of Libraries, 1973

Cawelti, John. *Adventures, Mystery, and*

Romance: Formula Stories in Art and Popular Culture. Chicago: University of Chicago Press, 1976

____. *The Six-Gun Mystique.* Bowling Green, Ohio: Popular Press, 1971

Clary, Mike. "Writers Who Also Steal Good Stories," *Akron Beacon Journal,* Oct. 27, 1984

Clauss, J.E. *Louis L'Amour Checklist.* Amereon, Ltd., 1987

Crider, Bill. "Louis L'Amour," *Dictionary of Literary Biography Yearbook.* New York: Scribner's; 1980; 240-245

Darrach, Brad. "Out of the Pages," *People,* June 9, 1975, 64-65

Etulain, Richard W. "Louis L'Amour," *A Bibliographical Guide to the Study of Western American Literature.* Lincoln: University of Nebraska Press, 1982. 181-182

Fields, Howard. "L'Amour Receives Congressional Medal," *Publishers' Weekly,* Oct. 14, 1983, 17

Fraser, C. Gerald. "How An Author's Pen Wins West," *New York Times,* May 23, 1975, A3

Gale, Robert L. *Louis L'Amour.* Boston: Twayne Publishers, 1985

Gardner, Bill. "Is Louis L'Amour Any Kind of Name for a Cowboy?" *The Detroit News*, March 31, 1978

Garfield, Brian. *Western Film: A Complete Guide*. New York: Rawson Associates, 1982

Gelb, Alan. "In Short," *New York Times Book Review*, July 6, 1984, 14

Gonlazlez, Arturo F. "Louis L'Amour: Writing High in the Bestseller Saddle," *Writer's Digest*, 60 (Dec. 1980), 22-26

Gottschalk, Earl C., Jr. "Eggheads May Shun Novels by L'Amour; Millions Love Them," *Wall Street Journal*, Jan. 19, 1978, 1, 31

Haller, Scot. "The World's Five Best-Selling Authors," *Saturday Review*, 8, (19, 20 March, 1980), 14-16

Halliwell, Leslie. *Halliwell's Film Guide*. Fourth Edition. New York: Charles Scribner's Sons, 1983

Haslam, Gerald, ed. *Western Writers*. Albuquerque: University of New Mexico Press, 1974, 69-89

Hawkins, Reese. *Scrapbook*. 2 Vols. At Alfred Dickey Library, Jamestown, N.D. Unpublished

Hinds, Harold E., Jr. "Mexican and Mexican-American Images in the Western Novels of Louis L'Amour," *Latin American Literary Review*, 5 (Spring-Summer, 1977), 129-141

House, Dick. "Santa Rosa, '81!" *The Roundup*, 29, 1981, 3-4

Hubbell, John G. "Louis L'Amour—Story-teller of the Old West," *Reader's Digest*, 117 (July 1980), 93-98

Jackson, Donald Dale. "World's Fastest Literary Gun: Louis L'Amour," *Smithsonian*, 18, 2 (May 1987), 154-170

Kalter, Suzy. "Louis L'Amour: He Tells How the West Was Really Won," *Family Weekly*, June 10, 1979, 4, 7

Keith, Harold. "Louis L'Amour: Man of the West," *The Roundup*, 23 (Dec. 1975), 1-2, 4, 12; 24 (Jan. 1976), 8-9, 11; 25 (Feb. 1976), 4-5

Klaschus, Candace. *Louis L'Amour: The Writer as Teacher*, Ph.D diss., University of New Mexico, 1983. Unpublished

_____. *The Frontier Novels of Louis L'Amour*, Master's thesis, San Francisco State University, 1978. Unpublished

Leerborn, Charles. "A Rare Breed of Writer," *Newsweek*, July 14, 1986, 88

Marsden, Michael T. "A Conversation with Louis L'Amour," *Journal of American Culture*, 2 (Winter 1980), 146-58

____. "The Concept of the Family in the Fiction of Louis L'Amour," *North Dakota Quarterly*, 46 (Summer 1978), 12-21

____. "Introduction" to *Hondo*, Boston: Gregg Press, 1978. v-x

____. "L'Amour, Louis (Dearborn)" *Twentieth-Century Western Writers*. Ed. by James Vinson. Detroit: Gale Tower, 1982. 471-78

____. "Louis L'Amour," *Fifty Western Writers: A Bio-Bibliographical Sourcebook*. Ed. by Fred Erisman and Richard W. Etulin. Westport, Conn.: Greenwood Press, 1982. 257-267

____. "The Modern Western," *Journal of the West*, 19 (Jan. 1980), 54-61

____. "The Popular Western Novel as Cultural Artifact," *Arizona and the West*, 20 (Autumn 1980), 203-214

McDowell, Edwin. "Everyone's Writing About Mr. Dooley," *New York Times*, Feb. 267, 1981, C22

____. "Louis L'Amour," *New York Times Book Review*, March 22, 1981, 34

_____. "Publishing: Congress Honors Louis L'Amour," *New York Times*, Sept. 23, 1983

Milton, John R. "The Novel in the American West," *South Dakota Review*, 2 (Autumn 1964), 56-76

Mitgang, Herbert. "Publishing: From Iran Into Hard Cover," *New York Times*, April 4, 1980

Moritz, Charles, ed. *Current Biography*. New York: H.W. Wilson Co., 1980. 203-206

Nesbitt, John D. "Change of Purpose in the Novels of Louis L'Amour," *Western American Literature*, 13 (Spring 1978), 65-81

_____. "A New Look at Two Popular Western Classics," *South Dakota Review*, 18 (Spring 1980), 30-42

_____. *Literary Convention in the Classic Western Novel*, Ph.D Dissertation, University of California, Davis, 1980. Unpublished

_____. "Louis L'Amour—Paper Maché Homer?" *South Dakota Review*, 19 (Autumn 1985), 37-48

_____. "Louis L'Amour's Pseudonymous Works," *Paperback Quarterly*, 1980, 3-6
Newsweek, 86 (Nov. 10, 1975), 86, 103

New York Times, May 28, 1975, 43

North Dakota Motorist, March-April, 1972, 4

North Dakota REC Magazine, July 1981, 12

Nuwer, Hank. "Louis L'Amour: Range Writer," *Country Gentleman*, 130 (Spring 1979), 99-100, 103

_____. Review of *Rivers West. Western American Literature*, 11 (Summer 1976), 167

Pearson, Richard. "Epic Western Novelist Louis L'Amour, 80, Dies," *Washington Post*, June 13, 1988, E6

Pilkington, William T., ed. *Critical Essays on the Western American Novel*. Boston: G.K. Hall, 1980. 150-163

Pircher, Joseph. "Pages," *People*, July 23, 1984

Price-Root, Susan. "Driving Through the Old West, L'Amour's Novels Are Roadmaps," *US* (July 25, 1978), 28-29

Rawls, Wendell, Jr. "Westers' Readers Love L'Amour," *New York Times*, June 26, 1980

Reued, J.D. "The Homer of the Oater," *Time*, Dec. 1, 1980, 107-108

Reuter, Madalynne. "Louis L'Amour Sues Carroll & Graf," *Publishers' Weekly*, July 8, 1983

Ring, Frances. "Interview with Louis

232

L'Amour," *American West*, July-Aug., 1982, 48

Rogers, Tom. "Author Louis L'Amour Surveys His Range," *USA Today*

San Francisco Chronicle, Jan. 22, 1975, 16

Sashachari, Candadai. "Popular Western Fiction as Literature of Escape," *The Possible Sack*, April 1973, 5-8

Smith, Ned. "Louis L'Amour: He's No Rhinestone Cowboy," *American Way*, April 1976

Smovada, James and Forrest, Louis. *Century of Stories: Jamestown and Stutsman County*. Jamestown, N.D.: Fort Seward Historical Society, 1983

Sullivan, Jack. "In Short," *New York Times Book Review*, Aug. 2, 1987, 16

_____. "Westward to Stasis with Louis L'Amour," *Southwest Review*, 69 (Winter 1984), 78-87

Thoene, Bodie. "L'Amour of the West," *American West*, 19 (July-Aug. 1982), 46, 47, 68

Tuska, Jon and Piakarski, Vicki, ed. "Louis L'Amour," in *Encyclopedia of Frontier and Western Fiction*. New York: McGraw-Hill Book Co., 1983, 208-211

Walker, Don W. "Notes on the Popular Western," *The Possible Sack*, 3 (Nov. 1971), 11-13

———. "The Scholar as Mountain Man," *The Possible Sack*, April 1973, 16-17

Wall Street Journal, Jan. 19, 1978, 1

Walters, Ray. "Paperback Talk," *New York Times Book Review*, June 15, 1980, 31

Washington Post, March 5, 1978, 1

Whitledge, Fred C., ed. *The Hitching Rail*, 4 (Feb. 1973)

Widener, Sandra. "The Untold Stories of Louis L'Amour: The West's Best-Selling Writer," *Denver Post Empire Magazine*, 13 Feb., 1983, 8-12, 14

Wilkinson, Tracy. "Louis L'Amour Dies: Prolific Western Writer," *Los Angeles Times*, June 13, 1988, 1, 14

Yagoda, Ben. "L'Amour Rides the Range," *Esquire*, March 13, 1979, 22

Zimmerman, Paul D. "Winner of the West," *Newsweek*, Nov. 10, 1975, 103-104

H. Selected Filmography

Hondo (Wayne-Fellows, 1953)
Director, John Farrow
Producer, Robert Fellows

Screenwriter, James Edward Grant
Cinematographer, Robert Burks/Archie Stout
Starring John Wayne, Geraldine Page, Ward Bond, Leo Gordon, James Arness

Four Guns to the Border (Universal, 1954)
Director, Richard Carlson
Screenwriter, George Van Marter/Franklin Coen
Starring Rory Calhoun, Walter Brennan, Colleen Miller, George Nader, Nina Foch, Charles Drake, John McIntire

Stranger on Horseback (United Artists, 1955)
Director, Jacques Tourneur
Producer, Robert Goldstein
Screenwriter, Herb Meadow, Don Martin
Cinematographer, Ray Bennahan
Starring Joel McCrea, Miroslava, John McIntire, Kevin McCarthy, Emile Meyer, John Carradine

Blackjack Ketchum, Desperado (Columbia Pictures, 1956)
Director, Earl Bellamy
Producer, Sam Katzman

Screenwriter, Luci Ward/Jack Natteford
Cinematographer, Fred Jackman Jr.
Starring Howard Duff, Victor Jory,
Maggie Mahoney, Angela Stevens, Martin
Garrelaga, David Orrick

The Burning Hills (Warner Brothers, 1956)
Director, Stuart Heisler
Producer, Richard Whorf
Screenwriter, Irving Wallace
Cinematographer, Ted McCord
Starring Tab Hunter, Natalie Wood, Skip
Homeier, Ray Teal, Earl Holliman,
Claude Akins

Utah Blaine (Columbia Pictures, 1957)
Director, Fred F. Sears
Producer, Sam Katzman
Screenwriter, Robert E. Kent/James B.
Gordon
Cinematographer, Benjamin Kline
Starring Rory Calhoun, Susan Cum-
mings, Max Baer, Ray Teal, Paul Langton,
Jack Ingram

The Tall Stranger (Mirisch, 1957)
Director, Thomas Carr
Producer, Walter Mirisch

Screenwriter, Christopher Knopf
Cinematographer, Wilfrid Cline
Starring Joel McCrea, Virginia Mayo,
Barry Kelley, Michael Ansara, Leo Gor-
don, Ray Teal

*Guns of the Timberland** (Warner Brothers,
1960)
Director, Robert D. Webb
Producer, Aaron Spelling
Screenwriter, Aaron Spelling/Joseph
Petracca
Cinematographer, John Seitz
Starring Alan Ladd, Jeanne Crain, Gilbert
Roland, Frankie Avalon, Lyle Bettger,
Noah Berry, Jr.
*Also released as *Stampede*

Heller in Pink Tights (Ponti-Girosi Produc-
tions/Paramount, 1960)
Director, George Cukor
Producer, Carlo Ponti/Marcello Girosi
Screenwriter, Dudley Nicholas/Walter
Bernstein
Cinematographer, Harold Lipstein
Starring Anthony Quinn, Sophia Loren,
Margaret O'Brien, Steve Forrest,
Edmund Lowe, Eileen Heckert

Taggart (Universal Pictures, 1964)
  Director, R.G. Springsteen
  Screenwriter, Robert Creighton Williams
  Starring Tony Young, Dan Duryea, Dick Foran, Emile Meyer, Jean Hale, David Carradine, Elsa Cardenas

Kid Rodelo (Trident Films, Fenix, 1966)
  Director, Richard Carlson
  Producer, Jack O. Lamont/James J. Storrow Jr.
  Screenwriter, Jack Natteford
  Cinematographer, Manuel Mering
  Starring Don Murray, Janet Leigh, Broderick Crawford, Richard Carlson, Jose Nieto, Julia Pena

Shalako (Kingston Films, a Dimitri de Grunwald Production, 1968)
  Director, Edward Dmytryk
  Producer, Euan Lloyd
  Screenwriter, J.J. Griffith/Hal Hopper/Scot Finch
  Cinematographer, Ted Moore
  Starring Sean Connery, Brigitte Bardot, Stephen Boyd, Jack Hawkins, Peter Van Eyck, Honor Blackman

Catlow (MGM, 1971)
 Director, Sam Wanamaker
 Producer, Euan Lloyd
 Screenwriter, Scot Finch/J.J. Griffith
 Cinematographer, Ted Scaife
 Starring Yul Brynner, Richard Crenna,
 Leonard Nimoy, Daliah Lavi, Jo Ann
 Pflug, Jeff Corey

The Sacketts (VHS II, 1982)
 Director, Robert Totten
 Producer, Douglas Netter
 Starring Glenn Ford, Tom Selleck, Sam
 Elliott, Ben Johnson, Gilbert Roland, Jeff
 Osterhage, Jack Elam, Slim Pickens,
 Mercedes McCambridge

ABOUT THE AUTHOR

Robert Phillips has published nearly twenty books, including biographical and critical studies of the Southwestern writer William Goyen and the English writer Denton Welch. His book, *Aspects of Alice: Lewis Carroll's Dreamchild*, has been published in four separate editions and is available in 44 countries. He is also the literary executor for the Estate of Delmore Schwartz, and has edited *Letters of Delmore Schwartz*, which met with acclaim. In 1988, Mr. Phillips was awarded the Arents Pioneer Medal by Syracuse University. He lives in Westchester County, New York, with his wife, Judith, and son, Graham.

WE hope you have enjoyed this
KNIGHTSBRIDGE book.

WE love good books just as you do,
so you can be assured that the
KNIGHT ON THE HORSE
stands for good reading, every time.